The Psychology of
money

WILEY FINANCE

Advanced Fixed-Income Valuation Tools, Narasimhan Jegadeesh and Bruce Tuckman

Beyond Value at Risk, Kevin Dowd

Buying and Selling Volatility, Kevin B. Connolly

Chaos and Order in the Capital Markets: New View of Cycles, Prices, and Market Volatility, Second Edition, Edgar E. Peters

Corporate Financial Distress and Bankruptcy, Second Edition, Edward I. Altman

Credit Derivatives: A Guide to Instruments and Applications, Janet Tavakoli

Credit Risk Measurement: New Approaches to Value at Risk and Other Paradigms, Anthony Saunders

Currency Derivatives: Pricing Theory, Exotic Options, and Hedging Applications, David F. DeRosa

Damodaran on Valuation: Analysis for Investment and Corporate Finance, Aswath Damodaran

Derivatives Demystified: Using Structured Financial Products, John C. Braddock

Derivatives for Decision-Makers: Strategic Management Issues, George Crawford and Bidyut Sen

Derivatives Handbook: Risk Management and Control, Robert J. Schwartz and Clifford W. Smith, Jr.

Derivatives: The Theory and Practice of Financial Engineering, Paul Wilmott

Dictionary of Financial Engineering, John F. Marshall

Dynamic Hedging: Managing Vanilla and Exotic Options, Nassim Taleb

The Equity-Risk Premium: Long-Run Future of the Stock Market, Bradford Cornell

Financial Statement Analysis: A Practitioner's Guide, Second Edition, Martin S. Fridson

Fixed Income Securities: Tools for Today's Markets, Bruce Tuckman

Fixed-Income Analysis for the Global Financial Market, Giorgio Questa

The Foreign Exchange and Money Markets, Second Edition, Julian Walmsley

Global Trade Financing, Harry M. Venedikian and Gerald A. Warfield

The Handbook of Equity Derivatives, Revised Edition, Jack Francis, William Toy and J. Gregg Whittaker

The Independent Fiduciary: Investing for Pension Funds and Endowment Funds, Russell L. Olson

Interest-Rate Option Models, Ricardo Rebonato

International M&A, Joint Ventures and Beyond: Doing the Deal, David J. BenDaniel and Arthur Rosenbloom

Investing in Africa: An Insider's Guide to the Ultimate Emerging Market, Justin Beckett and Micael Sudarkasa

Investment Management, Peter L. Bernstein and Aswath Damodaran

Investment Timing and the Business Cycle, Jon G. Taylor

Investment Valuation, Aswath Damodaran

M&A: A Practical Guide to Doing the Deal, Jeffrey C. Hooke

Managing Credit Risk: The Next Great Financial Challenge, John Caouette, Edward Altman, and Paul Narayanan

Managing Derivative Risks: The Use and Abuse of Leverage, Lilian Chew

Measuring Market Risk with Value at Risk, Pietro Penza and Vipul K. Bansal

New Dimensions in Investor Relations, Bruce Marcus and Sherwood Wallace

New Financial Instruments: Investor's Guide, Julian Walmsley

Option Pricing Models, Les Clewlow and Chris Strickland

Options on Foreign Exchange, Second Edition, David F. DeRosa

Options, Futures and Exotic Derivatives: Theory, Application & Practice, Eric Briys

Pension Fund Excellence: Creating Value for Stockholders, Keith P. Ambachtsheer and D. Don Ezra

Portfolio Indexing: Theory and Practice, Harold Hutchinson

Pricing Financial Instruments: The Finite Difference Method, Domingo Tavella and Curt Randall

Project Financing: Asset-Based Financial Engineering, John D. Finnerty

The Psychology of Money, Jim Ware

Relative Dividend Yield: Common Stock Investing for Income and Appreciation, Second Edition, Anthony E. Spare

Risk Arbitrage: An Investor's Guide, Keith M. Moore

Risk Management: Approaches for Fixed Income Markets, Bennett W. Golub and Leo M. Tilman

Security Analysis on Wall Street: A Comprehensive Guide to Today's Valuation Methods, Jeffrey C. Hooke

Style Investing: Unique Insight into Equity Management, Richard Bernstein

Using Economic Indicators to Improve Investment Analysis, Second Edition, Evelina Tainer

Valuation: Measuring and Managing the Value of Companies, Third Edition, McKinsey & Company, Inc., Tom Copeland, Tim Koller, and Jack Murrin

Value Investing: A Balanced Approach, Martin J. Whitman

The Psychology of
money

*An Investment Manager's Guide
to Beating the Market*

JIM WARE

John Wiley & Sons, Inc.
New York • Chichester • Weinheim • Brisbane • Singapore • Toronto

For my wife, Janey, who masterminds all
my work . . . I'm just the front guy.

This book is printed on acid-free paper. ∞

This publication is designed to provide accurate and authoritative information in regard to the subject matter covered. It is sold with the understanding that the publisher is not engaged in rendering professional services. If professional advice or other expert assistance is required, the services of a competent professional person should be sought.

Library of Congress Cataloging-in-Publication Data:

Ware, Jim, 1954–
     The psychology of money : an investment manager's guide to beating the market / Jim Ware.
          p. cm.—(Wiley finance series)
          ISBN 0-471-39074-7 (cloth : alk. paper)
          1. Investments—Psychological aspects. 2. Stocks—Psychological aspects. 3. Money—Psychological aspects. I. Title. II. Series.

HG4515.15.W37 2001   00-043608
332.6—dc21

3 2280 00772 7134

Printed in the United States of America.

10 9 8 7 6 5 4 3 2 1

preface

I think self-awareness is probably the most important thing to-wards being a champion.

—Billie Jean King

If you know yourself and your enemy, you will not fear battle. If you know yourself but not your enemy, you will lose a battle for every one that you win; and if you do not know yourself and do not know your enemy, you will never see victory.

—Sun Tzu, *The Art of War*

If you don't know who you are, the stock market is an expensive place to find out.

—Adam Smith, *The Money Game*

All business books claim to address and resolve a problem, and this one is no different. The problem examined here is that very few investment managers are beating their appropriate benchmarks. Professional money managers are not exceeding the returns that clients could get by investing in index funds. Simply put, money managers aren't adding value. And investors know it, which is why the index funds are growing.

So, what can money managers do to improve their competitive records? More of the same? If so, they would have fallen prey to the "streetlamp syndrome," captured in the story about the fellow who preferred to look under the streetlamp for his keys—rather than in the alley where he lost them—because the light was better under the lamp. These change-resistant money managers would also be guilty of behaving insanely, defined as follows: "doing the same thing over and over and expecting to get different results."

Instead, I suggest that money managers look in some new places. Specifically, they can look in the right sides of their own brains. The right side of the brain—which contains our skills in creativity, collaboration, and intuition—remains relatively untapped in the corridors of Wall Street. In fact, I was making just this point to Patrick O'Donnell, head of research at Putnam, when he remarked, "There is virtually no professional literature about managing creative investment professionals."

Surprised, I looked into it, and he was correct. There are tons of books on investment techniques and strategies, all presenting and advocating a particular viewpoint, but there are no books on managing the bright and creative individuals who run money professionally.

Thus the idea for this book was born. It is intended to fill an empty spot on the investment shelf. Mind you, there are lots of books on management in general and creativity specifically, but none that addresses the unique world of money management. In this sense, this book is the synthesis of my study and experience in three areas:

1. Professional money management (20 years as a Chartered Financial Analyst, finance instructor, and portfolio manager)
2. Psychology (Myers-Briggs Personality Type instructor)
3. Creativity (designed and delivered workshops on enhancing creativity; plus wrote, recorded, and released two music albums, a music video, and a novel)

The book is organized into four parts. The first part analyzes the investment traits of five past masters (Buffett, Lynch, Soros, Wanger, and Zweig). It discusses the eight great traits that each of these masters possesses and that account for their superior investment records. It then offers the reader some self-diagnostic tools to determine which of these personality traits could be identified and strengthened for the reader's benefit. In the course of this discussion, the reader is introduced to the Myers-Briggs Type Indicator (MBTI), a personality assessment tool that I use as a framework for much of the discussion about investment types. The part concludes with comments on whether there is an "ideal" investment personality and which personality is most common in the investment profession.

Part Two combines the Myers-Briggs framework with my experience in the money management field to examine the role of collaboration in the investment business. Tools and techniques are suggested to improve the effectiveness of teamwork. A case history is presented, in which portfolio managers using Myers-Briggs and consensus decision-making methods achieved superior results. The part concludes with applications of Myers-Briggs to the management of client relationships.

Part Three moves from collaboration to *creative* collaboration. It asks: "How can investment teams enhance their creative effectiveness?" A number of practical guidelines, using investment examples, are given. A premise of this book is that investors will have to be more creative than ever before to win in today's markets. (That's actually how this book came to be. An editor from John Wiley, Mina Samuels, heard me talk to professional investors on "The Role of Creativity in the Investment Profession" and decided it was a hot topic. We'll let you be the judge.)

The last part, entitled "The Intuitive Investor: Whole-Brained Investing," examines the evidence for using intuition as an equal partner with logic in the investment process. It concludes with a look at current practices of successful businesspeople who do rely on intuition to help them run their businesses.

Finally, this book is also meant to be fun. If you've been having way too much fun lately, and you need a big dose of seriousness, pick up one of the thick books on either side of this one, with lots of equations and a title like, "The Conservative Investor's Guide to Trading Derivatives: The Theory and Practice of Boring Your Competitors into Submission." That should balance you out a bit.

Enough said. Let the journey begin! May your enhanced creativity, collaboration, and intuition allow your portfolios to flourish.

JIM WARE

Glenview, Illinois
November 2000

acknowledgments

Thanks: To Judy Brownrigg at AIMR who got the ball rolling. To Mina Samuels at Wiley, who picked it up and ran with it. To Pamela van Giessen, who gracefully accepted the hand-off from Mina. To Jill Kneerim at Palmer & Dodge who kept the ball moving.

Thanks also to Dean LeBaron for his encouragement. And to various friends and colleagues at Interaction Associates, who provided stories and support throughout the process.

J.W.

contents

PART ONE

The Investor: Psychological Traits of the Masters

CHAPTER 1

Investment Masters: The Quintet   3

CHAPTER 2

The Eight Great Traits   9

1. Breadth: Taking in Information   9
2. Observation: Retaining Details   10
3. Objectivity: Thinking Clearly   10
4. Discipline: Being Consistent and Organized   12
5. Depth: Thinking in Focus and Independently   13
6. Creativity: Seeing the Big Picture and
   Using Metaphors   14
7. Passion: Maintaining Deep Devotion to the Subject   15
8. Flexibility: Being Open to Change, Going
   with the Flow   15

CHAPTER 3

Secrets of the Masters: Complexity   17

CHAPTER 4

Self-Diagnosis   23

Extravert (Breadth)/Introvert (Depth): The Energy Source   24
Sensing (Observation)/Intuiting (Creativity):
   What People Pay Attention To   26
Thinking (Objectivity)/Feeling (Passion):
   How People Make Decisions   28

Judging (Discipline)/Perceiving (Flexibility):
    How People Choose to Live   30
Self-Testing   33

CHAPTER 5
Strengthening One's Abilities: Drop and Give Me 50   **35**

Extraverts and Introverts: Stretching Exercises   36
Sensing and Intuition: Stretching Exercises   39
Thinking and Feeling: Stretching Exercises   42
Judging and Perceiving: Stretching Exercises   44
Striking a Balance   46

CHAPTER 6
The Ideal Investment Personality   **47**

CHAPTER 7
The Typical Investment Personality   **51**

PART TWO
The Investment Team: Collaborative Techniques

CHAPTER 8
Teamwork Today?   **67**

CHAPTER 9
Golden Gloves or Golden Rule?   **75**

CHAPTER 10
Tools for Investment Teams   **81**

Identifying Preferences   82
Getting a Team Working Together   84

CHAPTER 11
Case History: Collaboration for a Money Management Team   **89**

CHAPTER 12
Temperaments and Teams: Implications for the Markets   **97**

The Guardian (SJ): Lions Rule the Kingdom   100

The Rationalist (NT): The Wise Old Owl   102
The Adventurist(SP): The Wily Fox   103
The Idealist(NF): The Compassionate Dolphin   105

CHAPTER 13
Temperament and Client Service   **109**

PART THREE
The Creative Investment Team: Tools for Enhancing Creativity

CHAPTER 14
Brainstorming for the Masses   **121**

CHAPTER 15
The Creative Investor: Taming the Critics   **129**

CHAPTER 16
Creating a Safe Place   **139**

Exercises: Creating a Safe Place   148

CHAPTER 17
Guidelines for Safety   **151**

Exercise   157
Tools for Enhancing Creativity: "ACROBAT"   160

CHAPTER 18
"A" Is for Assume Nothing   **161**

Exercise 1: Overconfidence Quiz   166
Exercise 2: Clean Slate   167

CHAPTER 19
"C" Is for Change Gears   **169**

CHAPTER 20
"R" Is for Risking Discomfort   **175**

Exercise   179

CHAPTER 21
"O" Is for Omit Either/Or Thinking   **185**

Exercise   189

CHAPTER 22
"B" Is for Borrow from Other Disciplines   **191**

Exercise   193

CHAPTER 23
"A" Is for Ask for Help   **195**

Exercise   201

CHAPTER 24
"T" Is for Tools and Techniques   **203**

CHAPTER 25
Getting Personal   **213**

Exercise: What Kind of Investor Are You?   222

PART FOUR

The Intuitive Investor: Whole-Brained Investing

CHAPTER 26
Quantum Investing   **225**

CHAPTER 27
Waves and/or Particles   **231**

CHAPTER 28
The Case for Intuition   **235**

CHAPTER 29
Operating on All Cylinders   **241**

Index   **251**

The Investor: Psychological Traits of the Masters

CHAPTER 1

Investment Masters

The Quintet

The best thing that I did was to choose the right heroes.
—Warren Buffett

We start the journey by studying the habits of some investment masters. Habits are critical to success. Many of us have at some point been on a physical fitness jag. We do exercises, follow a certain diet, and set goals (weight, cholesterol level, etc.). Depending on our motivation level, we may even get the desired results. What often happens, however, is that we eventually fail because we cannot break our old habits. We still eat the sweets, butter the bread, skip the workout. Habits are extremely powerful forces in our lives. One psychologist, Earnie Larsen, estimates that as much as 98 percent of our behavior is governed by habits (Larsen, *Stage II Recovery*, HarperCollins 1985). The point here is that unless we change our habits, our exercise program will have little effect. And if we expect to get different results from doing the same thing over and over, then we are fooling ourselves. Remember the definition of insanity: doing the same thing repeatedly and expecting different results. (For example, mixing SlimFast with Ben & Jerry's ice cream for your diet breakfast.)

Money managers fall into this "habits" trap all the time. They experience disappointing results at year end and resolve on New Year's Day that they will do better in the coming year. How? By doing the same things, but more so. They dig faster and deeper in the same dry hole. Why? Because we learn as kids: If at first you don't succeed, try, try again. Also, mediocre performance tends to makes us a bit nervous (read: pink slip). So, we tighten up and push for results. Studies show us that this pressing limits our flexibility and makes us less likely to try new things. We revert to our most predictable behavior.

Humans love routine, especially when we are under stress. Like lizards that dart out from under a rock, catch a fly, and dart back to safety, we figure out a routine that works and follow it religiously. Edward DeBono, a leading expert on creative thinking, asserts that the biggest myth about creativity is that humans are naturally creative (DeBono, *Serious Creativity*, HarperCollins 1992). We aren't. We are creatures of habit. So this is where the definition of insanity applies. Investors must be willing to examine their results and ask, "Is my approach working?" If not, something must change. A mental fitness program for investors would involve identifying and changing unproductive habits.

What would such a program look like? Success in investing depends on the quality of our thinking. That is the skill a superior investor brings to the table. Michael Jordan brought superior physical skills (great agility and great eyesight); Elle McPherson has great physical beauty; Warren Buffett has superior decision-making skills based on his quality of thinking. What components of Buffett's thinking produce these superior decisions? He reads the same financial press and studies the same finance and investment concepts as most other investors, but somehow he takes those ingredients and bakes a better lasagna. How does he do that?

This book explores that question and offers a mental fitness program for improved results. For those of you who like step-by-step, one-size-fits-all formulas, I'm sorry—no can do. As with physical fitness, each person's program must be tailored to his or her own body and health. But I can explain the concepts so that you can start to tailor your own program.

Returning to the question, "How does he do that?" I chose not only Buffett but also four other investment masters to study. I looked for common threads in their thinking styles, so that useful generalizations could be made. The chosen five had to meet three criteria:

1. They had to have exemplary performance records over a long period of time.
2. There had to be enough information available about them so that I could understand and analyze their thinking styles.
3. Their investment approaches had to be sufficiently different from the other four.

The last factor was included because I didn't want the discussion to end up focusing on the old investment chestnut of growth versus value. (It might devolve into a beer debate: less filling, tastes great, less filling, tastes great . . .)

What approach is superior in investing? Evidence indicates that many approaches can win in the market, assuming that the investor has superior decision-making abilities. Figure 1.1 shows the five money masters and their records and approach.

	Return/Period	*Approach*
Warren Buffett	25.4% (1968–1998)	Value
Peter Lynch	31.3% (1977–1988)	Growth
George Soros	34.0% (1969–1988)	Trader
Ralph Wanger	17.2% (1970–1998)	Themes
Marty Zweig	16.0% (1985–1995)	Technical

FIGURE 1.1   The masters, their records, and their approaches.

Each of these investors is widely accepted as a master. The question is, what do they do differently? What habits have they acquired that lead to a superior quality of thinking? Can their thinking be replicated?

The premise of this book is that these investors share eight habits in their thinking style, which, in turn, lead to superior results. Can we ordinary mortals do it? Well, there's good and bad news there: Yes, we can understand and copy it, but not easily.

We live in a culture that promotes instant everything. Faster computers, faster Internet access, faster food service. As with physical fitness programs, this mental fitness program requires a genuine commitment to achieve any real gain. Those who have made that commitment, though, have seen the benefits.

Successful investing, then, is the result of superior thinking combined with a reasonable approach. Different approaches can win in the market. The question becomes this: What qualities or habits do the truly successful investors share? Underneath their educational training, advanced degrees, IQs, and so on, what underlying factors separate them from the rest of us?

Buffett himself says that the differentiating factor is *not* IQ. And most of us have heard the old joke about Einstein in heaven, where he is asked to share a room with three others:

Einstein to first roomie: "What's your IQ?"

First roomie: "150."

Einstein: "Great, we can talk about relativity theory and quantum mechanics."

Einstein to second roomie: "What's your IQ?"

Second roomie: "120."

Einstein: "Good. We can talk about literature and the arts."

Einstein to third roomie: "What's your IQ?"

Third roomie: "75."

Einstein: "Oh. Well, how did the market close today?"

IQ and creative genius are clearly different. Many brilliant investors fail, whereas some with ordinary IQs succeed. Richard Feynman, an excellent model of creative thinking, remarked that it wasn't such a big deal to win the Nobel prize—lots of people had done that. What was a big deal, though, was his winning it with an IQ of only 128! Again, IQ and creative genius are unrelated.

Without further delay, let's look at the eight habits that these master investors share.

CHAPTER 2

The Eight Great Traits

Habit is habit, and not to be flung out of the window by any man, but coaxed downstairs a step at a time.

—Mark Twain

Don't you hate those books—with titles like "The Secret to Prosperity: Investing in Bull Markets"—that take a simple concept and stretch it over five lifetimes? I read one recently where the author's point was that leadership involves managing opposing forces—like the interests of shareholders versus the interests of employees. Valid point, but it didn't require 281 pages to pound it into my brain. So in this chapter, I present the guts of my findings . . . briefly. That way there will be room for some other neat material in the book and you'll still be able to finish this by the time the plane lands. Here are the eight great traits of master investors.

1. BREADTH: TAKING IN INFORMATION

Breadth refers to a person's ability to take in data. Like radar that constantly scans the horizon, these five investors are ravenous for information. Their interests include not only domestic common stocks, but foreign stocks and other asset classes—and interests outside of investing as well. Soros, for example, was a philosophy major and is deeply involved in world politics. Lynch is involved in charitable causes.

Consider Peter Lynch's schedule when he was actively managing the Magellan Fund. He visited with about 50 managements per month, which meant more than 500 per year, traveling more than 100,000 miles. When not traveling, he received upwards of 50 broker calls per day and timed each one with an egg timer. Each salesperson had 90 seconds to make the pitch. Why? Because Lynch was hungry for more information. He wanted to free up the line for the next blip on the radar screen.

2. OBSERVATION: RETAINING DETAILS

Sherlock Holmes once remarked to Watson, "You see, but you do not observe." What the legendary detective meant, of course, was that Watson did not see the significance of the small clues, the ones that unlocked the mystery. Again, all five of the masters share this capacity for details. This trait is different from the first (breadth). Two analysts might go to the same conference, but one would come away with a wealth of important details, whereas the other might retain very little. Retention of details, then, is key to successful investing. Ralph Wanger remarks, in his book *A Zebra in Lion Country* (Simon & Schuster 1997), that most research is just plain hard detail work. Likewise, Buffett is famous for his encyclopedic knowledge of the facts. He is able to recite the financial condition of all the businesses in his home town of Omaha, as if their balance sheets were printed on the facades of their buildings.

3. OBJECTIVITY: THINKING CLEARLY

The behavioral finance people have explored this area rather thoroughly, discussing such phenomena as overreaction, overconfidence, anchoring, and the like. Their point is that the economic assumption—that humans are rational decision makers—is false. Rather, we make systematic errors in our thinking that lead to predictable and exploitable investment mistakes.

The most powerful example of this in my experience occurred in 1989. Iben Browning, a climatologist for PaineWebber, predicted that a major earthquake would strike northern California in the fall. Iben was a great presenter, a good storyteller with provocative subjects: earthquakes, tidal waves, and volcanoes. I cannot remember any of his predictions coming true, but he followed the adage: often in error, never in doubt. (My own guess about Iben's position at PaineWebber is that the firm's economists wanted him on board to make their economic forecasts appear more credible.) Rather surprisingly, Iben's prediction about the quake in Northern California proved accurate. Immediately thereafter, Iben's stock as a forecaster shot up. The *Wall Street Journal* carried a story about him and his accurate prediction. Soon he issued another warning: that the New Madrid fault, which runs through St. Louis and the Midwest, would shift later that year. (This event was not unprecedented; in the nineteenth century an earthquake occurred in that area and shook church bells as far away as Boston.)

Iben predicted a similarly shocking blast. Closer to home, the news of this prediction began to affect my colleagues in Chicago, all of whom were professional investors and most of whom had advanced degrees and designations like Chartered Financial Analyst (read: intelligent). One by one these intelligent professionals bought earthquake insurance. That's how strong panic mania can be. Of course, having studied behavioral finance and learned about our tendency to succumb to irrational fears, I was able to resist much longer than most before calling my insurance agent, Arnie.

Me: "Arnie, can you give me a quote on earthquake insurance?"
Arnie: "On what?"
Me: (softly) "Earthquake insurance."
Arnie: "I've never quoted that before. Just a second."

Returning after a few moments:
Arnie: "How would you like to buy some *deep mining* insurance?
Me: "What is that?"
Arnie: "Well, if someone is mining near your house and they set off an explosive that damages it, then your house is covered."
Me: "Why would I want that?"
Arnie: "Well, it's cheaper than earthquake insurance, and since you won't need either, I thought I'd save you some money."

As you know, of course, the joke was on my colleagues and me. We got pulled into the panic mentality, believing that there might be an earthquake. There never was. But the point is about objectivity and how hard it is to maintain. Dostoevsky, the great Russian novelist, was of the opinion that you can say anything you want about human beings, but don't say they are rational. Behavioral finance people agree.

Despite the difficulty of remaining objective, Soros is known to be cool as ice under pressure, even when the stakes are high. As Lynch is fond of saying, "The stock doesn't know that you own it, so don't take it personally."

4. DISCIPLINE: BEING CONSISTENT AND ORGANIZED

This trait is so important that several firms use it in their advertising. One firm proclaims, "Solid Performance Built on Discipline, Consistency, and Teamwork." Zweig, the technician, agrees. He instructs investors never to "fight the tape." In his book, *Marty Zweig's Winning on Wall Street* (Warner Books 1997), he gives examples of the times when Jesse Livermore (his idol) went against this wisdom and regretted it.

Similarly, Buffett believes that the secret to investing is—to use a baseball metaphor—swinging at the perfect pitch. Wait for the fat one; don't flail away at all the wild, crazy noise in the market. That is discipline. Hence his suggestion that each new investor be given a card with 20 punches on it. He believes that each investor will probably only have 20 or so great ideas in a lifetime of investing. So, wait for them.

Lynch admits that in his career he has fallen off his path several times. He says that he's fallen for about 30 whisper stock recommendations. (These are the mysterious phone calls where someone whispers the name of a hot stock. Lynch comments: "Don't they realize that the SEC can amplify these conversations?") In any event, all of these stocks went bad for Lynch, reminding him yet again that he needed to stick with his strategy of extensively researching the management and business and learning the "story" behind the stock.

5. DEPTH: THINKING IN FOCUS AND INDEPENDENTLY

The French mathematician Pascal once remarked that most of the world's troubles are caused by the inability of men to sit quietly in a room. This dictum can be applied to many investment analysts. How many of us can shut the door and think deeply and independently, rather than falling under the influence of what others say? The trait of depth acknowledges the importance of such thinking. Soros is known to permit no distractions when he is working. He is said to have unremitting concentration. It is this sort of focus that allows him to develop and implement winning trading strategies.

Similarly, Richard Feynman, the Nobel prizewinner mentioned earlier, made the same request when he started teaching physics after his work in Los Alamos on the atom bomb. He asked for several hours of uninterrupted time each morning so that he could think deeply and do the kind of thought experiments that Einstein had already made famous.

6. CREATIVITY: SEEING THE BIG PICTURE AND USING METAPHORS

A recent issue of *Forbes* magazine contained 12 ads for financial firms, all stressing their creative edge. Success in today's rapidly changing world requires innovation at all levels: portfolio selection, asset allocation, marketing, recruiting, and so on. Ralph Wanger, one of our masters, is a fan of the metaphor as a creative tool. He encourages analysts to use metaphors to play with their ideas and avoid "hardening of the categories." Furthermore, Wanger believes that intuition is a valuable ally, especially when it is developed through experience on the job. (More on intuition later.)

Also important is humor. Humor is a sign of a creative mind. These masters all have their own brand of wit, revealing their creativity. Lynch playfully speaks of finding great investment ideas in the malls, where his wife—who has a black belt in shopping—accompanies him. He quips that if you spend 13 minutes a year studying economics, you've wasted 10 minutes. And he tries to find companies that any fool could run, because eventually one will. A playful mind won't get hardening of the categories.

Similarly, Buffett is renowned for his dry sense of humor. He says that one strategy for increasing sales at Sees Candy stores was to spread the rumor that the candy is an aphrodisiac. It worked wonderfully. (The rumor, that is, not the candy.) He also writes that he and his partner, Charlie Munger, can compose a four-page memo with three grunts on the telephone. He bounces his ideas off Munger, who always tells Buffett that they are dumb. When Munger says they are *really* dumb, then Buffett reconsiders; but when they are evaluated as merely "dumb," then he takes that as a vote of confidence and goes forward. He says of his relationship with Munger that they will be working together for many years to come, until eventually one day they look over at one another in the office and think, "Who is that guy sitting over there?"

The humor in these remarks reveals a playfulness that allows these masters to take their ideas lightly, to change their thinking when appropriate. They can step back and see the bigger picture.

7. PASSION: MAINTAINING DEEP DEVOTION TO THE SUBJECT

Master investors love the subject. They enjoy the journey more than the destination. Buffett jokes about enjoying the process more than the proceeds, though he says he has learned to live with the proceeds as well. He adds that he tap-dances into work each day. Zweig reveals that in college, when he began studying the markets, he fell in love with the numbers. Appropriately, he ended up as a technician, deeply involved with and working with the numbers. The market gods seem to favor investors whose motivation is from the heart, not greed. (Gordon Gekko aside, many master investors become active philanthropists.) Importantly, in the late 1980s, when Lynch stopped loving the market, he made the wise decision to get out. He knew the importance of passion and withdrew from active management when his own waned.

8. FLEXIBILITY: BEING OPEN TO CHANGE, GOING WITH THE FLOW

One portfolio manager friend was recently told by an exasperated colleague, "Do you know that you always answer a question with a question?" My curious friend responded, "Really? Is that bad?" (Okay, it was me.) Along with their capacity for creativity, these master investors also have the ability to remain open to new data and new paradigms. They are slow to shut the door on new possibilities, knowing that they might miss something important if they rigidly pursue a fixed strategy. Soros, a trader, is renowned for his ability to change on a dime. (Sometimes several billion dimes, in a

Breadth (taking in information)	**Depth** (focusing intently on one company)
Observation (taking in the details)	**Creativity** (seeing the big picture, themes)
Objectivity (able to be clear and unemotional)	**Passion** (deep devotion to subject)
Discipline (decisive and organized)	**Flexibility** (open to change, go with flow)

Figure 2.1 The eight traits of the masters.

single day.) He calls his system a flexible theoretical framework that can accommodate any global economic development. Likewise, Zweig says that the single reason why most investors fail to win in the markets is because they are not flexible.

Those are the eight traits that emerged as I read and studied the styles and strategies of these five masters. I've listed them in Figure 2.1 and have positioned them in a particular fashion. Does anything jump out as you look at these traits? Do you see a pattern? (Can you remember which of the eight traits helps you to spot patterns?)

Some of you probably noticed that these traits are positioned as opposites, as polar extremes. It brings to mind the definition of mixed emotions: like watching your mother-in-law go over a cliff in your new Cadillac. The ability to move between extremes is what distinguishes the investment masters—and what makes creative genius a tricky proposition. For this reason, the next chapter is entitled . . .

CHAPTER 3

Secrets of the Masters

Complexity

I get the facts, I study them patiently, I apply imagination.
—Bernard Baruch

Like Michael Jordan, who shoots and dribbles with either hand, these investment masters can go both ways. Similarly, Leonardo da Vinci is rumored to have been able to write with both hands simultaneously. Most of us, alas, can only do one at a time. The significance of this fact, as it relates to the eight traits, should not be underestimated. It helps explain why there are so few masters. They are masters precisely because they have the capacity to excel at both extremes. In a study on creative genius done by Professor M. Csikszentmihalyi at the University of Chicago, he found that this capacity to cover both extremes explains much of what we understand to be genius:

> If I had to express in one word what makes [geniuses'] personalities different from others, it would be *complexity*. By this I mean that they show tendencies of thought and action that in most people are segregated. They contain contradictory extremes—instead of being an "individual," each of them is a "multitude." Like the color white that includes all the hues in the

spectrum, they tend to bring together the entire range of human possibilities within themselves.

These qualities are present in all of us, but usually we are trained to develop only one pole of the dialectic. We might grow up cultivating the aggressive, competitive side of our nature, and disdain or repress the nurturing, cooperative side. A creative individual is more likely to be both aggressive and cooperative, either at the same time or at different times, depending on the situation [M. Csikszentmihalyi, *Creativity*, HarperCollins 1996].

When I talk about this subject to groups, they get a funny look at this point. It's an expression that says, "Hmmm, there's more to this than I originally thought." The eight traits are not simply a laundry list of rituals to be completed, like flossing, brushing, and gargling. A dynamic tension exists within each of the four scales.

For example, the second scale, observation versus creativity, pits logical, linear, and detailed thinkers against creative, intuitive, and big-picture thinkers. Both forms of thinking are valuable, but it is difficult to be good at both, and quite impossible to be good at both simultaneously. (It's a bit like the Magic Eye pictures that shift from two- to three-dimensional and back again as you stare at them.) Typically each of us has a preference for one type of thought or the other, much like left- and right-handedness; people are born with a preference for one hand or one type of thought over the other. In fact, to illustrate this point with a group, I ask them each to write their name on a sheet of paper. No big challenge, right? People do it effortlessly, without thinking. Then I ask them to write it again with the opposite hand. Usually there are a few audible groans and some laughter. It's difficult, and for those of us who like to be masterly at all times, it's kind of embarrassing. But eventually everyone does it. If necessary—say, if he or she broke the dominant hand—a person could become skillful with the opposite hand. Normally, though, we don't even think about the choice of hands; we just sign checks with our "usual" hand.

There is a way that these two different ways of thinking—

observation and creativity—show up in investing. When I ask investors, "What do you like in the market?" they typically reveal their preference in their answers. The detail-oriented, linear thinkers tend to give a response like this: "I like Merck right now. The company's earnings per share have been growing at 13 percent over the past five years. Return on equity is 44 percent for the past year. The current P/E multiple is 28.7x, which compares favorably with the market average. They have three new products coming on the market that look promising, and their debt-to-equity ratio is under 10 percent. Earnings per share next year are expected to increase to $2.80 from $2.45."

Contrast that response with this one from a creative, big-picture type: "I like the play on the graying of America. The baby boomers are aging and will require more prescription drugs. So, a natural play is the pharmaceutical companies."

Notice the language in each response. The first is literal and factual: "13 percent," "44 percent," "28.7 multiple." The second response is figurative and conceptual: "graying of America," "baby boomers are aging." In traditional investment dialect, the former is known as a "bottom-up" approach: Start specific and work to the general. The latter is known as a "top-down" approach: Start with the overview and work down to specifics.

To revisit our sports analogies, Michael Jordan had to develop complexity in his basketball game. He was born with a preference for one hand over the other (in his case, right-handedness). It would have been easier for him simply to become a right-handed dribbler and shooter, but he knew that he would never dominate the NBA with only "half" his weapons. Therefore, he worked tirelessly on developing his "weaker" side.

Likewise, master investors must become equally skilled from both sides of the brain. They must fire on all eight cylinders, which is another way of saying that they must master complexity. Many of us have well-developed preferences for one or the other poles, but not equal facility with both—and that is why we fail to achieve superior results. Sherlock Holmes said, "My peculiar art of detection results from the interplay of reality and imagination." He meant that he had both observational and creative abilities. He could take in the facts and then play with them to see beyond them to the truth that we "Watsons" cannot perceive.

To give a sense of how complexity plays out with our master investors, Figure 3.1 shows some examples of them going to each polar extreme.

Without an understanding of complexity, the statements in the figure are confusing. The masters appear to be speaking out of both sides of their mouths. (Sort of like the man who said, "I used to be schizophrenic, but we're better now.") Their statements make

Soros: Breadth/Depth	"[C]onstantly reading newspapers and talking to well-placed sources around the world."	"Unremitting concentration"; "permits no distractions."
Buffett: Observation/Creativity	"[Can] rattle off the financial characteristics of every building and business he passes in town."	"I look for businesses in which I think I can predict what they're going to look like in 15 or 20 years."
Lynch: Objectivity/Passion	"The stock doesn't know that you own it. Don't take it personally."	"Obsessed with stocks"; "[y]ou won't get there if you don't love it."
Zweig: Discipline/Flexibility	"Discipline is the key; never fight the tape."	"The problem with most people who play the market is that they are not flexible."

Figure 3.1 Complexity through opposition.

sense only in the light of complexity. When viewed this way, they are showing that they can dribble with either hand, or—to use a tennis metaphor—that they can hit a backhand and a forehand equally well.

Some investors have asked me, "How well do these traits hold up in the decade of the 1990s?" After all, Peter Lynch hasn't been actively managing money this past decade. Furthermore, a *Forbes* article, entitled "Quit While You're Ahead" (February 7, 2000), states that Lynch's approach—buy what you are familiar with—wouldn't have worked in the 90s. The article uses Lynch's picks from *Worth* magazine during the 90s and concludes that his selections would be valued as "27% less than identical sums put into the S&P 500."

Ouch. Say it ain't so!

Buffett is another case in point. He often mocks himself for not understanding technology and hence not investing in it. Modesty aside, his portfolio picks have suffered as a result of his techno-phobia. Blue-chip growers like Coke just can't compete with the likes of Microsoft and AOL.

So, are these eight traits outdated? Or are there contemporary all-stars who demonstrate them?

I believe the traits are alive and well. In fact, I like them for this very reason. Regardless of cycles or fads, yuppies or Gen-Xers, the deep truths of life remain the same. As you will see in Chapter 4, the eight traits are based on deep truths about our psyches. But to make my point, consider a modern superstar, Mike Lu.

Mike Lu manages the Janus Global Technology Fund. This fund was up—brace yourself (especially if you didn't own it)—212 percent in 1999. In that same period, average technology funds climbed 135 percent. The S&P 500 increased 21 percent. Lu is considered a superstar by his coworkers.

Does he practice the eight habits? It seems so. His radar screen is constantly searching for ideas, both in and out of the investment field. He studies politics, architecture, and automotive design. He frequently corrects coworkers on details in their areas of expertise. (I didn't ask him if he has been punched out for this yet.) Also, he meets with lots of companies and attends conferences that target technology developers. Thus, he seems to have a broad perspective.

What about depth? Lu has excellent powers of concentration and is soft-spoken, a common trait of introspective, deep thinkers. He reads continuously. His capacity for independent thought is remarkable, according to his colleagues.

He seems to cover both poles of the observation/creativity scale, too. He has a photographic memory for details and openly states that he likes the nitty-gritty. But—on the other extreme—he also loves to be up on the latest innovations and newest trends.

Lu seems to have a clear preference for objectivity, as the president of his high school computer club and an economics major in college. But he also has a deep passion for learning and excellence, which he attributes to his parents' influence.

Finally, then, on the scale of discipline/flexibility, Lu is patient and disciplined about the way he puts money to work. He doesn't trade often and he won't throw new money at standard names simply to get money in the market. Moreover, Lu has shut the fund to new investors to keep it small and agile. On the flexible side, it goes almost without saying that anyone who follows technology has to be flexible, with technologies coming and going overnight.

With only one sensational year under his belt, it is hard to judge Lu a master yet. Nevertheless, his use of complex thinking suggests that he may be on track to achieve lasting success.

If complexity is the key to the masters' success, then how does one develop this quality of thinking? How do we strengthen our mental backhands and forehands so that we can hit from both sides? Or, to use a mechanical metaphor, how do we tune our engines so that we can fire on all eight cylinders?

There is a well-known and researched tool from psychology that can help.

CHAPTER 4

Self-Diagnosis

It is not paradox to say that in our most theoretical moods we may be nearest to our most practical applications.
—Alfred North Whitehead

Fortunately, there is a tool that can help in the process of attaining complexity in thinking. The Myers-Briggs Type Indicator (MBTI), which has been around for more than 50 years and has been taken by more than 10 million people worldwide, measures these same polarities in thinking. First conceived of by psychologist Carl Jung, the MBTI was developed into the practical tool that we use today by Katherine Briggs and her daughter, Isabel Myers.

The tool measures the way we prefer to use our minds. Similar to left- and right-handedness, each of us has a preference for one extreme of the polarities mentioned in Chapter 3. An example: Some analysts prefer their offices to be neat and tidy, with a place for everything; others live in the midst of huge paper piles. Neither is correct, they are just different. Investors with each style have succeeded.

Here are the four polarities that we've already discussed in "investment" terms, presented in Myers-Briggs language.

EXTRAVERT (*BREADTH*)/INTROVERT (*DEPTH*): THE ENERGY SOURCE

The first polarity deals with a person's energy source. Introverts tend to recharge their batteries alone or in the company of only one other person. Research shows that introverts tend to have more internal activity (thinking) going on, so external input (conversations, images) can overload them fairly quickly. Young children exhibit differences in behavior in this regard. Introverts will pick up a toy and play with it exclusively for a long time, sometimes to the point of becoming overwhelmed (i.e., bursts of tears, tantrums). Extraverted children, in contrast, will switch from one toy to another, seemingly gaining energy as they do so. Extraverts are enlivened by people, places, and things. They like being where the action is. Their chief fear is missing something if they are isolated. Conversely, introverts fear losing *themselves* if they are out in the world too much.

Some words associated with each type are:

Extravert (E)	Introvert (I)
Breadth	Depth
Interaction	Concentration
Do-think-do	Think-do-think
Outside thrust	Inside pull

An example of an extravert in the world of politics is John F. Kennedy: energetic and outgoing, a gifted communicator with large audiences. In contrast, his opponent, Richard Nixon, was more introverted: thoughtful, slower to respond, and less comfortable with crowds.

In the world of entertainment, Robin Williams is a screaming extravert, whose thought processes are on display for all to see. (A friend's advice to Williams was, "It's okay to have an unexpressed thought!") Another very funny man, but with an introverted style, is Woody Allen. In the few interviews that Allen grants, he is low-key and pensive. He thinks for a moment before he responds, following the introvert's pattern of "think-do-think."

Extraverts tend to choose careers like sales or politics; introverts choose ones like research or science. About 55 percent of the population is basically extraverted, 45 percent introverted.

Now that you have a feel for the difference, test yourself by assigning a type to the originators of the following quotations. Are the speakers likely to be extraverts or introverts?

> "Honors and rewards fall to those who show their good qualities in action." (Aristotle)
> "I never worry about action, but only about inaction." (Winston Churchill)
> "The world is too much with us." (Emily Dickinson)
> "Most of the world's troubles are caused by the inability of men to sit quietly in a room." (Blaise Pascal)

The first two are extraverts, right? The emphasis is on action and the world. The second two are introverts, with the focus on solitude and the inner world.

In investment terms, the extraverts like to visit with managements, go to conferences, talk on the phone, and sit in bullpens. They are good at collecting data and gathering information. Their weaknesses may well be concentration, depth of thought, and independent opinion. (A puppy can concentrate for about three seconds, then it's bored or distracted.)

Conversely, introverts like to study research reports, work on their computers, and write memos. They are good at concentrating and thinking carefully through an idea. Their weakness may be isolation—not enough contact with the real world. They can become lost in their thoughts and theories, failing to check them out in everyday life or to put them into any kind of action. (Sometimes they can go an entire day without noticing that a pen has leaked in a shirt pocket. . . .)

SENSING (*OBSERVATION*)/INTUITING (*CREATIVITY*): WHAT PEOPLE PAY ATTENTION TO

This second polarity describes what we pay attention to. Do we prefer to collect facts through our five senses or to "play" with the facts in our imaginations? Sensing types are realistic and place their trust in what they can touch and see. Intuitives get bored with the details and like to dream up new approaches and new theories. They enjoy future possibilities more than current realities.

Words that describe each preference are:

Sensing (S)	Intuiting (N)
Practical	Theoretical
Facts	Inspirations
Step-by-step	Leaps of intuition
Perfecting skills	Learning new skills

A famous sensor (S) would be Jimmy Carter, with his engineering background. His critics used to complain that he was too involved in the details to see the bigger picture. In contrast, Albert Einstein, the physicist, was a famous intuitive (N). He once said that "imagination is more important than knowledge." His approach to physics reflected this emphasis on imagination: in his famous "thought" experiments, he would dream up theories and then "test" them in his mind. Another famous scientist, Nikola Tesla, is also known for this mental ability. He would construct experimental machines in his mind and then let them run until the apparatus wore out! (The imagined machines, that is, not his brain.) He could literally test equipment in his mind.

A pair of clear opposites were featured in the entertainment world's popular movie and TV series, *Star Trek: The Next Generation*. Data, the android, was a perfect sensor. He retained all the facts and used his computer brain to organize them in perfect linear fashion. Counselor Deanna Troi, a Betazoid, represented the opposite extreme. Her species had intuitive powers of empathy, enabling her to read people's feelings. This polarity between Data and Troi was illustrated at the beginning of one episode as the two were playing three-dimensional chess. In the scene, Data questions one of Deanna's moves as being illogical, to which she responds that intuition can be a very powerful tool and should not be underrated. Data looks puzzled by her response. Sure enough, though, after her next turn, Data concedes matter-of-factly (he has no emotions) that she will checkmate him in three moves.

Sensing types prefer careers as actuaries, accountants, or "hands-on" professionals (such as carpenters or mechanics). Intuitives prefer big-picture work and often become strategists, architects, or creative writers. Almost two-thirds of the population are sensors, with the remaining third showing a preference for intuition.

Here are some quotes from sensors and intuitives. See if you can guess which type the speakers were.

"A foolish consistency is the hobgoblin of little minds . . ." (Ralph Waldo Emerson)

"Ultimately, speed of innovation is the only weapon we have." (Andy Grove, Intel Corporation)

"Just the facts, Ma'am." (Sgt. Joe Friday, *Dragnet* television series character)

"God is in the details." (Mies van der Rohe, architect)

Right. The first two are the intuitives, preferring the big picture; the second two are sensors, trusting the facts and details.

For investors, the sensing types (observers) prefer methods of research and valuation that rely on facts and established relationships. Their motto—like a blend of Sergeant Joe Friday and Jerry Maguire—is "show me the facts!" They don't like hunches or new paradigms; they *do* like what has worked over the years. Their weakness is often the inability to anticipate change. They are not likely to buy the dot.com stocks, because these stocks defy traditional valuation methods. Intuitive types (creators), in contrast, love playing with new ideas and theoretical abstractions. They are the ones who build the elaborate computer models and develop elegant theories like "efficient markets." Never mind that they aren't real—they're fun to dream up! The weakness of intuitive types is that they get too far removed from reality and invent impractical models, or they come up with ideas that are "ahead of their time." (And suffer the consequences that Bert Lance referred to when he said, "Pioneers get the arrows!")

THINKING (*OBJECTIVITY*)/FEELING (*PASSION*): HOW PEOPLE MAKE DECISIONS

After people have taken in data and played with some options, there comes a time for decisions. By what process do people make final decisions? Some tend to decide in a logical, detached way, that is, thinking. These people prefer to look for an outside reference point, such as a law or standards or a formula, which will allow them to pass judgment objectively. These people tend to focus on tasks over people and may be thought of as tough-minded. Their weakness may be the inability to see how decisions affect human relationships and conditions. The feeling types focus on subjective decisions. They are often frustrated by laws and standards and make statements like, "Yes, that's the law and it doesn't make any sense!" (Like 55-mile-per-hour speed limits for wide-open highways on clear sunny days!) They prefer to go within themselves to their own value systems, their own personal standards, and determine what seems right subjectively. (65 MPH seems just fine, thank you.) They focus on people first, tasks second. They tend to be perceived as tender-hearted. Their weakness is that they can be seen as arbitrary or inconsistent by coworkers.

Words that describe each of these types are:

Thinking (T)	Feeling (F)
Logical system	Value system
Justice	Mercy
Critique	Compliment
Principles	Harmony

Two famous generals, one on the battlefield in World War II and the other on the battlefield of civil rights, represent the thinking/ feeling polarity. General Patton, hero of the European theater of war, was the tough-minded thinker. Dr. Martin Luther King, Jr., also had a war to fight, but his preference for feeling caused him to choose a very different approach. Following the practices of Gandhi, King believed that the only way to freedom was non-violence.

The thinking/feeling polarity was also highlighted in the original Star Trek television show. Mr. Spock, the ultralogical Vulcan represented the consummate thinker, whereas "Bones" McCoy, the ship's doctor, was the compassionate feeler. The writers of the show used these characters to show the conflicts that often arise between thinkers and feelers.

The population is evenly distributed between thinkers and feelers, although this is the one scale that reveals a gender bias. About 60 percent of men prefer thinking, and 60 percent of women prefer feeling.

This preference for thinking or feeling has nothing to do with intelligence (IQ). Thinkers often pursue advanced degrees in law or finance, whereas feelers tend to choose advanced degrees in psychology or education.

Here are some classic lines from thinkers and feelers:

"I think, therefore I am." (René Descartes, philosopher)
"I think that I think, therefore I think I am." (Ambrose Pierce, writer)

"You may say anything that you like about mankind, but don't say it is rational." (Dostoyevsky)

"I never met a man I didn't like." (Will Rogers)

"Will Rogers never met a lawyer." (Steve Moris, entertainer)

Clearly, two thinkers, two feelers, and a comic.

In practice, most investment professionals (more than 90 percent) show a preference for thinking. They tend to be competitive and tough-minded. When a hurricane strikes Florida, they tend to think about the investment ramifications (lumber futures, citrus crop damage, and insurance stocks) rather than dwell on the human suffering caused by the event. Their capacity to be objective helps them to see clearly and eliminate emotion from their decisions. This same objectivity can damage working relationships and drive down morale in their organizations.

Feeling types tend to make excellent client advisors and marketing professionals, as they can use their natural inclination to see things from another person's perspective. Their weakness shows up when they need to make tough decisions that may result in confrontation or hard feelings.

JUDGING (*DISCIPLINE*)/PERCEIVING (*FLEXIBILITY*): HOW PEOPLE CHOOSE TO LIVE

The final polarity deals with people's lifestyle. Judging types like an orderly, organized life. Their idea of freedom is to have a clear idea of where they are going and then be free to achieve it. They don't like long brainstorming sessions; they would rather decide on a plan. Once the plan is in place, they can relax and get to work. They like to set goals and achieve them. They like DayTimers and planners. Their weekends are booked and to-do lists are common. In fact, they cannot believe that anyone functions differently. As I explained these distinctions to the senior staff at Uline Corporation, the president jumped from her chair and said, "Do any of you NOT plan your weekends?" She was astonished to find that half of her staff did not.

The opposite extreme is the perceiver. This person likes to go with the flow. The perceivers like to remain open to last-minute information or changes, and to investigate all the possibilities. They hate planning their weekends. They prefer to do whatever they feel like, when they feel it. The television show *The Odd Couple* was a play on this polarity. Oscar and Felix were perfect opposites in this way: one messy, one neat. Here's one way to determine which is your preference: What were your study habits in school? Did you start early and read an assignment each week for six months, or cram during the last two weeks before the exam? If you were an all-nighter type, then your preference is for perceiving.

Here are some words that describe each type:

Judging (J)	**Perceiving (P)**
Control	Adapt
Closing off	Opening up
Organized	Flexible
Set goals	Seek options

A more modern pair of TV stars who represent these opposite polarities are from the show *Frasier*. The father in the show, Martin Crane, is an easygoing guy who likes to lounge in his comfy old chair. His son, Niles, is just the opposite. He dresses immaculately, fusses over appearances, and uses a pair of tweezers to pick undesirable elements off his breakfast muffin.

Slightly more than half the population shows a preference for judging. These types tend to like jobs with closure and definition, like trading securities, where a trade is completed and done quickly. Another career choice for judgers would be quality control expert, inspecting to make sure that everything is just so. (I couldn't believe it when I learned that my cousin arranges his dollar bills in his billfold so that all the presidents face the same direction. I know, it's not wrong, it's just so . . . so anal-retentive!)

Perceivers like jobs that give them flexibility and room to negotiate. A diplomat or improvisational comedian is likely to have a "P" preference.

See if you can pick the judgers and perceivers from the following quotes.

"Sit loosely in the saddle." (Robert Louis Stevenson)

"Life is what happens while people are making plans." (John Lennon)

"Life is tons of discipline." (Robert Frost)

"Man must be disciplined for he is by nature raw and wild." (Immanuel Kant)

Two perceivers, followed by two judgers, right?

Investment types tend to be more judging than perceiving, especially in the trading rooms, where decisions must be made and executed without much hesitation. The strength of judging types in the investment world is their ability to bring order to the chaos of the markets, to impose their valuation systems on seemingly random occurrences. Their capacity to be decisive even in the midst of uncertainty and high pressure can be extremely valuable. I remember a senior officer at Drexel Burnham Lambert who, during the market crash on October 19, 1987, bought heavily at noon—a very gutsy and decisive move—only to see the Dow drop several hundred more points in the next few hours. Decisive and wrong.

The perceiving types in the investment world are valuable as researchers, who will forever dig and uncover more data because they are unwilling to settle for a partial picture. Their weakness, of course, is that they can go forever without reaching a conclusion or taking any action. Like the fabled two-handed economist, perceivers tend to say, "On the one hand . . . but on the other hand . . . " Another interesting aspect of judgers and perceivers is their attitude toward money itself. Judgers tend to be conservative and like saving; perceivers are more risk-loving and like spending.

If you are still having trouble determining whether you have a preference for judging or perceiving, consider the state of your office or home. Figures 4.1 and 4.2 are photos of professional money managers, whose offices are next to each other. One manages foreign stock funds, the other convertible preferred stocks. Which most closely resembles your living space? Is there any question about their preferences!?

SELF-TESTING

Based on the preceding discussion, do you have a sense now of your own four preferences? Try to determine your four preferences.

FIGURE 4.1 The "organized" office (J preference).

FIGURE 4.2   The "flexible" office (P preference).

Got them? If not, you can go to any number of Myers-Briggs
Websites and take the MBTI formally. The quickest one—it's free—
is found at <www.haleonline.com/psych/>. The importance of
knowing your type will become more evident as we move away
from theory and discuss the practical applications of the MBTI.
Sensing types will be delighted to know that the next chapters deal
with real-life applications; that is: How can I use this stuff?

CHAPTER 5

Strengthening One's Abilities

Drop and Give Me 50

The nature of man is always the same; it is their habits that separate them.

—Confucius

Remember the premise of this book: Master investors have earned their title by developing skill at both ends of the spectrum. Their ability to run on all eight cylinders gives them the competitive edge. The question is, then, what can we ordinary investors do to improve our game?

First off, we can learn our own preferences so that we know ourselves as investors. We can only improve our personal performance, and that of our team, from the vantage point of self-knowledge. The Myers-Briggs Type Indicator helps in this regard. It allows individuals to see clearly how they are "hardwired."

The next step is to interpret the results from the perspective of improving investment performance. This step is similar to golfers or tennis players analyzing their weaknesses and then working with a coach to improve their putting or serving. The difference is that a golfer usually knows his weakness (putting, sand traps, driving, etc.), whereas a money manager may have no idea what the weakness in his "mental game" is or how to strengthen and overcome it. That's the value of the MBTI. It helps us get beyond the fact that "we don't know what we don't know." In fact, a recent study, reported in the *New York Times*, suggested that the very people who are most confident of their skills are the ones who are least competent:

> In a series of studies, Dr. Kruger and Dr. Dunning tested their theory of incompetence. They found that subjects who scored in the lowest quartile on tests of logic, English grammar and humor were also the most likely to "grossly overestimate" how well they had performed.

The study relates to investors in this way:

> This deficiency in "self-monitoring skills," the researchers said, helps explain the tendency of the humor-impaired to persist in telling jokes that are not funny, of day traders to repeatedly jump into the market—and repeatedly lose out—and of the politically clueless to continue holding forth at dinner parties on the fine points of campaign strategy" (*New York Times*, Jan. 18, 2000).

How can that be? Apparently, you need to have some competence in an area before you can even begin to judge your own abilities.

The following are "exercises" for each of the functions, so that investors can strengthen their weaker areas.

EXTRAVERTS AND INTROVERTS: STRETCHING EXERCISES

Extraverts love action and are energized by people, places, and things. As investors they like to kick the tires. Peter Lynch seems to have a natural preference for extraversion, as seen in his constant traveling and visits with managements. Lynch is known for finding his ideas at the malls, by getting to the stores and seeing them firsthand. Here is an example of his regret at not getting out in person to see a new company:

> In hindsight, I wish I had dragged myself out to the Chestnut Hill Mall to visit the new NordicTrack retail store. I would have seen firsthand the array of new products—the NordicFitness chair, the NordicFlex Gold body building machine, NordicRow TBX, the recumbent bike exerciser, and the various advancements in stationary skiing.
>
> If I had watched the customers try out this equipment, perhaps I would have understood the importance of these retail outlets, which by 1992 accounted for about 25% of NordicTrack sales. Perhaps I would have taken Skip Wells's megatrend projections more seriously ["When the Peter Lynch Rule Fails," *Fortune*, Oct. 25, 1999].

The "stretch" for extraverts is spending more time alone, concentrating on the numbers and data. This is difficult for extraverts because they feel that they are missing something when they are off by themselves. Their tendency is to go to a conference, attend a management lunch, or talk on the phone. Almost any activity will do as long as it involves other people. (I remember telling my extraverted mother-in-law how excited I was—as an introvert—about going to a friend's farm, 200 acres of just quiet and solitude. Her response? A horrified "Borrrr-ing!") Extraverts join investment clubs and read *Barron's* in the café at Borders.

All of this is fine, except that the likelihood of original thinking is often reduced when one works with others. The behavioral finance people have shown that it is harder to remain unbiased than you might think. We are subtly influenced by the attitudes and opinions of others. One experiment that shows the power of these subtle influences asked people to guess the year of the Magna Carta signing: A.D. 1215. The participants were divided into two groups and were seated in separate rooms. In one room, the number 1435 was displayed on the blackboard. In the second room, the number 1100 was displayed. These numbers were never mentioned by the researchers. Rather, the participants were given a series of questions to answer, including the Magna Carta date. As you can probably guess, the participants in the room with the higher number on the blackboard had a significantly higher average answer than the group with the 1100 figure on the board. Without even being conscious of these numbers, the people in each room were influenced by them. Similarly, the amount of television we watch influences our perception of reality. People who watch lots of TV report that the world is much more dangerous than those who don't watch much TV.

An exercise for extraverts is to keep track of how much time they spend out in the world researching investment ideas versus the amount of time spent alone thinking and researching stocks. The balance between the inner and outer world is important to successful investing. The single biggest tool that we all possess to maintain the balance is awareness—simply paying attention. If we know our natural tendency and consciously work to balance it, we will be more likely to win in the markets. Do you know how much time you spend trying products and talking to people versus reading and thinking? Try keeping a diary for a week and check the ratio.

When I was an analyst following retail stocks in the late 1980s, one of the hottest names was The Limited. Everything they did seemed to work. Management was cocky. Growth was outrageous. Of course, the P/E ratio climbed to nearly twice the market level. Reading the reports and running the numbers, I could not find a way to make The Limited a buy recommendation. It was too expensive, based on my assumption that their "hot" streak would cool off in several years. We passed on the stock and thereby missed one of the biggest success stories of the decade. Moral: A wise man leaves the office and follows his kids around the mall.

Why did I make that call? Looking back at it now, I know it was my own preference for introversion. Given a choice, I'd rather stay in the office to read and think about companies than go to the mall and check them out. My reaction to the Limited situation was much like Lynch's reaction to missing CML's stock:

> One of the benefits of visiting a retail outlet is that it brings the numbers alive. You can study a company's earnings potential all day long, but bullish forecasts always seem more believable after you've seen the evidence in person at the mall. But I never gave myself a chance to view the evidence. I stayed at home and ignored all the positive signs, as CML's stock price rose from a low of $3.50 in late 1990 to $33 by the end of 1992 ["Best of the Best," *Worth Online*, Mar. 1998; <www.worth.com>].

Of course, personal visits don't always ensure huge gains. If they did, we'd all be exhausted from racing around to as many companies as our little legs could carry us. But in my case, I learned to ask myself if I was being prudent—saving time and money—by not visiting or just giving in to my preference for introversion. My stretch as an introvert was to balance the amount of time reading and studying reports with an equal amount of time kicking the tires. The combination of the two, which is what each of the masters has, is the winning balance.

SENSING AND INTUITION: STRETCHING EXERCISES

Consider the investor who discovers that she has a strong preference for intuition. She is wonderful with the big picture, themes, brainstorming new ideas, following complex theories. But she is much weaker in the sensing area. She doesn't dig for facts, and during management interviews often finds herself daydreaming about points that the CFO brought up 10 minutes ago. (As one intuitive friend said to me, "Facts are boring." Einstein was supposedly unable to remember his own phone number, and—when asked about it—would simply reply that there was no point in remembering facts that one could look up!)

What can our hypothetical investor do to strengthen her "S" function?

As with strengthening a muscle, she can do some exercises or activities that strengthen the sensing function. Any activity that forces her to be in the present moment will do this. For example, tennis forces her to be in the moment as she follows the flight of the ball. Juggling or roller-blading or skiing would work, also. The point is to focus the mind on what is happening right now. (Remember the mantra of the 1960s: Be here now?)

Another exercise is any activity that forces the investor to notice and retain useful details. As an intuitive, I (should) practice this when I play bridge. It takes a considerable amount of attention for me to count cards. My intuitive preference loves surprises and new possibilities. I don't really *want* to know who's holding which card; it actually takes the fun out of the game for me to "know" what cards are still left to be played. Contrast this with the attitude of a good "sensor," who loves to know with mathematical precision the exact location of each card.

A final exercise for strengthening the sensor function is to follow carefully the directions for setting up a new piece of electronic equipment (e.g., stereo, VCR, computer). Rather than just tearing into the box and guessing where the cords plug in, open the directions and read them, step by step. (At this point, sensing types will be asking themselves, "You mean there are people who *don't* do that?!" Yes. The intuitive motto is: If all else fails, then read the directions.)

Flip it around. What if you have a strong preference for sensing? You are great at uncovering facts and reasoning in a linear fashion. Here are some exercises for strengthening the "N" muscle.

Next time you have a business problem, pose it to five coworkers. Listen to their suggestions, then find the common themes in their ideas. The point here is to exercise your ability to see patterns and discern general themes. Imagine what solution you could develop from their responses that would get all their heads nodding in agreement.

Here's another exercise that may sound far-fetched, but I've used it successfully with corporate executives. Ask the participants to pick someone—real or legendary—who represents wisdom to them. Then have them imagine a dialogue with this wise figure. You might say, "Ask the figure, in your mind's eye, for suggestions on your problem. Let the wise person respond, rather than giving your own conscious answer." Some people prefer to do this by writing it out. Scientists and inventors have used techniques like this to tap into their intuition. A colleague of mine once sat next to Lear, inventor of the Lear jet and the eight-track tape. He asked how Lear had invented all these different products. Lear responded that he used the "universal mind." *"What's that?"* my friend said. Lear said that, as a teenager, he had read that all ideas resided in a universal mind (something like Jung's idea of the collective unconscious) and that all one needed to do was "drop in" to this mind and look at the answers! This story sounds like something from the *X-Files*, but my friend swears it is true. And there's no denying that Lear has come up with some unusual inventions.

One of the most frequently recommended techniques for tapping into intuition is to learn a simple meditation technique, such as the relaxation response studied by Herbert Benson, a Harvard M.D. (this is meant to persuade the sensing and thinking types who are a bit skeptical of anything mystical and want some evidence and credentials). The idea in meditation is to shut off outside distractions so that one can tune in to that "wee small voice" that the Quakers speak of. The mystics tell us that the mind is strongest when it is still. ("Be still and know that I am God.") Meditation helps quiet the mind.

Edison's method of tapping into the unconscious was novel. He seemed to know that the unconscious was a precious source of creative solutions, so he devised the following strategy. He would sit in a comfortable chair with rocks in his hands and pans on the floor under the rocks. Then he would doze off. The rocks would fall, hitting the pans and waking him. He would try to recall where his thoughts had been as he drifted off to sleep. Author Sandra Weintraub reports that her surveys of inventors show that 75 percent use their dreams to invent new products. Skeptical sensing types need to open themselves up to the reservoir of knowledge that is "hidden" within. I will have more to say on this in Parts 3 and 4, the chapters on creativity and intuition.

THINKING AND FEELING: STRETCHING EXERCISES

A portfolio manager I know, who has a strong preference for thinking, is extremely good at making objective decisions. Even if the investments involve highly charged issues like natural disasters or birth control products, he is excellent at discerning the key variables. He sees the situations as purely logical, one thing leading to the next, and bases his decision on potential profitability. This ability to detach is captured in Peter Lynch's description of a cancer insurance company:

> As the new products begin to pay off, cancer insurance is less important to the bottom line. In 1993, noncancer policies accounted for 68 percent of AFLAC's new domestic sales. Taking a lesson from its Japanese operations, AFLAC is selling these new policies through payroll deduction plans, to companies that range in size from 2 or 3 employees to 10,000 ["Company after My Own Heart," *Worth Online*, Mar. 1994; <www.worth.com>].

The gruesome effects of cancer are irrelevant to Lynch's analysis. This objectivity is very effective in investing. The problem for thinking types occurs when the emotions flare up, as they inevitably do. An example with a colleague, the portfolio manager mentioned earlier, makes the point. He had bought a large position in an initial public offering (IPO) of PharMor (a discount drug retailer). For a while he looked like a hero. Earnings were impressive. The stock moved up nicely. But then news turned negative on the stock and the price plunged. It turns out that the company had acted fraudulently. The manager exploded, taking it as a personal affront: "How could they have lied to me, those bastards!" Given his rather low "emotional intelligence" quota, he stomped into the trading room and told them to sell the entire position. Even though the traders, who had cooler heads, showed some concern about his order, he paid no heed and blew out his entire position, several million dollars, in an afternoon. That volume of stock drove the price down further as traders reacted to his orders. In short order, though, the stock rebounded and returned to its trading range. By reacting emotionally, this portfolio manager cost his firm more than $200,000. That's an expensive emotional indulgence.

Similar incidents occur repeatedly in trading rooms around the country. Panic, fear, and anger take over and poor trades are the result. Even the most primitive of solutions—say, a "buddy system" in which a portfolio manager would have to run the trades by his or her buddy—would help eliminate these costly reactions. One of the advantages of investment clubs and chat rooms is precisely this ability to filter out the emotion from the decision. Intuition can be a positive ally, but emotion typically is not.

The real danger is that most professional investors are thinking types and would overestimate their score on Daniel Goleman's emotional intelligence test. Much like the Dunning research (*New York Times*, Jan. 18, 2000), which shows that we all overestimate our abilities, I've found this to be true of investors. In training workshops ranging from communication skills to diversity issues, investors tended to overrate their own abilities.

Investors with a preference for feeling need to balance in the other direction. They need to cultivate their capacity for objectivity. An exercise for them could be to watch a grisly news story and simply pick out the facts. Then try to logically explain the flow of causation in the story. What was the chain of events? Successful investors react to world disasters with a detachment that seems unconscionable. Again, imagine Mr. Spock from *Star Trek* and his logical mind. He focuses on the goal and which steps will lead there most efficiently, leaving out the human emotion factor.

Another exercise that feeling types could try would be a list of pros and cons. Instead of using gut-feel to make a decision about a stock pick, write down the pros and cons. Write down your rules for buying stocks. See if the particular stock meets the criteria you've selected. Make the exercise as precise and mathematical as you can. Show it to a strong thinking type and see if it makes sense to her. Does the conclusion follow logically from the premise?

JUDGING AND PERCEIVING: STRETCHING EXERCISES

The final scale is characterized in the vernacular as anal-retentive versus slob; think Felix and Oscar in *The Odd Couple*. The strength of the former is organization and discipline; the latter's strong suits are flexibility and openness.

The weaknesses are apparent. Judging types can be too rigid, too attached to the old ways. Many articles in the financial press lately have pointed out that the old valuation techniques don't work anymore. People who buy AOL or eToys aren't playing by the same old rules. The inability to change can hurt performance significantly. The *Wall Street Journal* ran a story about a mutual-fund manager who uses a value approach to stock selection. He looks for "cheap" stocks. His portfolio has been underperforming and the money in his portfolio has shrunk from nearly $8 billion to about half that in two years. When asked about the high-flying technology stocks, Mr. Sanborn's reaction is typical of someone with a preference for judging: "The thought of buying such overpriced shares is something that I'll never do . . . . It's like having a religion" (*Wall Street Journal*, Jan. 3, 2000).

Similarly, Zweig, one of the masters, agrees that we should never "fight the tape." Yet Zweig also says that the biggest reason why novice investors fail is their inability to be flexible. So which is it? Actually, it's the proper *mix* of the two, which we've defined as *complexity*.

The other side of the coin—from judgers and their strict adherence to a certain discipline—is perceivers who waffle between disciplines. I've worked in firms where the portfolio managers chased the latest fad, always seeming to be a day late and a few hundred million short. As sectors of the market come in and out of favor, the perceivers invariably jump on too late and get off too late, missing the excess returns and wondering why this pattern feels so familiar. (Because, as perceivers, they've probably done it a dozen times before.) The trick for perceivers is to establish some methods for discipline and stick to them. Perhaps not rigidly, but enough to establish a pedigreed rather than mongrel investing style.

Another area where perceivers can undermine their own best efforts is in simple organization. Earlier in the book (Chapter 4) we showed a picture of two offices, of a judger and a perceiver. Despite what perceivers may say about their "unique" filing systems, most of the time more organization would help these folks make better decisions. Organization, far from blocking creativity, adds to it. The goal is to establish an environment of contained chaos, an orderly mess. Too much chaos or too much order saps the energy and creativity from the process. Decisions become routine and reflect the safety of the herd.

Accordingly, judgers and perceivers can each stretch a bit in the other direction to round out their abilities. Judgers can skip planning their weekends and just go with the flow. Or take a driving vacation and follow their noses, ending up wherever the spirit takes them. In the decision-making process, they can practice remaining open to new ideas beyond their comfort zone. Wait 10 extra minutes before saying, "Okay, let's make some buy decisions and give the orders to the trading desk."

Perceivers need to spend some time getting organized, putting some structure around their natural chaos. In my case, I hired an organization coach. (I call her the "commandant"; she is merciless.) Perceivers also need to be conscious of deadlines and the urgency that market trading demands. (I remember working with one analyst who provided absolutely the most thorough research I had ever seen. The problem was that it was usually several days after the stock in question had moved.) Perceivers need to work on the 80/20 rule so that they can close down an investigation before they've researched every last question: Get the gist of it (the 80 percent) and move on.

STRIKING A BALANCE

For all the polarities, the right amount of one versus the other is the magical quality that we might call *wisdom*. The first step to attaining that wisdom is recognition and understanding of the different choices. Simply put, investors need to become conscious of the decision process.

Now that we've established a way of looking at the investment decision process, and done some consciousness-raising, let's focus on the next question: What is the ideal personality style for the professional investor?

CHAPTER 6

The Ideal Investment Personality

The most important quality for an investor is temperament, not intellect. You don't need tons of IQ in this business. You don't have to be able to play three-dimensional chess or duplicate bridge. You need a temperament that derives great pleasure neither from being with the crowd nor against the crowd. You know you're right, not because of the position of others but because your facts and your reasoning are right.

—Warren Buffett

When I give talks on personality styles and investing, people ask, "Is there an ideal personality type for managing money?" I confess that when I first started researching the personality styles of master investors, I got very excited about this question. Was there a possibility of finding an "ideal" type for money management? What if Warren Buffett and Peter Lynch were the same personality type? What if investment firms could recruit portfolio managers based on their type? Sound far-fetched?

In the professional sports arena, a man named Niednagel is doing just that. Simply by watching a player walk and talk, Niednagel can determine which position he should play. An article by Martin Dugard in *American Way* magazine (Dec. 15, 1998) reports that Niednagel is a consultant to Phoenix Suns coach Danny Ainge. When asked about a trade with Dallas that brought Jason Kidd to the Suns, Niednagel gave Ainge the following advice, "He's an ISTP. They're your ideal NBA point guard. They have great peripheral awareness. They conserve their energy well. They're great thinkers. When they play under control and see the floor well, they have the potential to make the whole team better. Michael Jordan's an ISTP."

Well, there's the clincher. You just can not argue against Air Jordan.

In any event, Niednagel gets big bucks from managers to help with draft selections, based on the Myers-Briggs Type Indicator of the players. I fantasized: What if I could do the same thing with MBA graduates for Goldman Sachs or Merrill Lynch? What if I could put on my MBTI turban and predict which eager MBAs were most likely to shine in the markets?

Perhaps there would be more than one ideal type. Maybe there would be one for trading, one for analysis, one for risk arbitrage. I was hopeful, so I dug in and read everything I could find about the masters. But my hope faded as I read more about the personality types of the masters and realized that they differed. I shifted to a new hypothesis: These masters achieved greatness because they understood their own personality type and used an investment approach that was congruent with it.

Of course, that was it. Socrates and Shakespeare were right after all: Know thyself and then to thine own self be true. One investment writer, Derrick Niederman, has already written a book, *The Inner Game of Investing* (Wiley 1999), that elaborates on this theory. He does not base it on the MBTI, but instead describes investment styles that he invented: The Bargain Hunter, The Visionary, The Contrarian, The Sentimentalist, and so on. It's a fun book, a good airplane read—but I wasn't satisfied with Niederman's "to thine own self be true" theory either.

As I continued to study the masters, it became obvious that

they were more than just good at their "own thing." They exhibited the quality of complexity or genius that Csikszentmihalyi wrote about in his book on creative genius (see Chapter 3). The masters can move to either extreme of the polarities, one minute thinking in broad, big-picture concepts, the next minute picking nits in an earnings report to see if the footnote explains an accounting change. Eventually, I abandoned the notion that one personality style was better for investing success than another.

All personality styles can be winners in the market, but they must understand their own strengths and weaknesses and compensate accordingly. This sort of self-knowledge leads to wisdom and personal mastery. The five experts that I've chosen to discuss have demonstrated abilities in all eight of the Myers-Briggs preferences: sensing and intuiting, judging and perceiving, and so forth. Later in this book, then, we will deal with the preference that seems most difficult for all of us: creativity and intuition.

For now, though, let's ask another question about personality types: Which one is the most *typical* for investors?

CHAPTER 7

The Typical Investment Personality

Nothing is more suicidal than a rational investment policy in an irrational world.

—John Maynard Keynes

Within this framework, then, is one type of investor more common than another? Does the profession attract a certain breed of animal? (And is it housebroken?) If there is a stereotypical investor, does that have certain implications for the industry?

Yes, yes, sometimes, and yes.

The most common personality type for professional investors is Sensing, Thinking, and Judging (STJ), in MBTI jargon. (There is no clear majority on the Extravert/Introvert scale, with each preference being about equally represented.) My own experience in working with investment groups (more than 500 individuals) supports this "STJ" assertion. Experts in the field of psychology also support this view:

> "If you had to brand fund managers with psycho jargon, they'd be **STJ** on the widely used Myers-Briggs personality test." (Ted Bililies, psychologist)

"Finance and administration are very likely to be **STJ** departments." (William Bridges, author)

The implications for the industry are profound. In fact, some evidence suggests that a major shift is occurring. Firms that are unaware of the shift may end up on the scrap heap of mutual funds.

First off, STJ personalities are very one-sided in their thinking, based on the famous left–right brain hemisphere work done by Roger Sperry. (He received the Nobel prize for his research and discovery of the bicameral brain functions.) This means that STJ types tend to be detail-oriented, logical, precise, efficient, decisive, and organized. Sounds pretty powerful, right? Robert Moore, a well-known Jungian analyst, thinks so. He calls these types "lions." They are typically very effective and powerful people. They are "go-to" people who can get the job done. They have a take-no-prisoners attitude and tend to rise to leadership positions. In fact, as Figure 7.1 shows, most United States Presidents have been STJ personalities.

So far, so good. Most investment leaders are lions, and lions tend to be natural leaders. So what's the problem?

Balance is the problem. The common theme running throughout this book is the importance of the golden mean; nothing in excess. Lions naturally favor the left brain. So, to bring the whole brain into play, they need to compensate for this preference by strengthening the right side. Herein lies the problem.

Consider a piece of research that I've conducted with groups. I've divided the lions (left-brainers) and the jesters (right-brainers) into their respective groups and asked them to discuss their strengths and weaknesses. When they report back on strengths, the lions have no trouble listing them: detail-oriented, logical, decisive, and so on. The jesters usually report: creative, intuitive, open-minded, adaptable, and so on. Both groups are then asked to consider their weaknesses. The jesters come back with a long list: flaky, dreamy, too sentimental, deadline-dysfunctional, and others. Now, here's the interesting finding: When the lions are supposed to report their

Myers-Briggs Type (based on temperaments described in next section)	*STJ* Sensing-thinking-judging	*SP* Sensing-perceiving	*NT* Intuitive-thinking	*NF* Intuitive-feeling
Number of Presidents	21	13	6	0
Examples	Washington Wilson Truman Nixon Ford Carter Bush	Roosevelt Kennedy Johnson Reagan Clinton	Adams Lincoln Grant Hoover Eisenhower	

Figure 7.1 MBTI classifications of U.S. Presidents.

weaknesses, they stare at one another, furrow their brows, and shrug their shoulders. No weaknesses.

At first blush, this response may seem highly arrogant or simply naïve. However, consider it in the context of our society, which loves efficiency and productivity. Ever since we were tiny children we've been rewarded for neatness, timeliness, coloring inside the lines, finishing the exam first, getting the right answer—all the things at which left-brainers naturally excel. So, of course, they tend to think that they're doing life "correctly."

Roger Sperry, the originator of the left–right brain theory, believes that there is a huge untapped resource for most people in the right hemisphere, as a result of this societal emphasis: "Our educational system and modern society generally discriminate against one whole half of the brain. In our present educational system, the attention given to the right hemisphere of the brain is minimal compared with the training lavished on the left side."

Increasingly, research is validating the importance of the interplay between the left and right brain. For example, a new form of psychological treatment called Eye Movement Desensitization Reprocessing (EMDR) is based on the interplay between the two hemispheres. It has proven very effective in treatment of trauma victims. Asking patients to move their eyes from left to right, which alternately stimulates the opposite brain lobes, has been very successful in releasing trauma experiences from the psyche. (Much of the early research was done with Vietnam veterans who had post-traumatic stress syndrome. The success rate was nearly 80 percent, versus less than 50 percent for all other forms of therapy.) The point? Our quest for flexible and effective thinking must include use of the whole brain, much like EMDR does in healing the psyche. Lions must overcome their comfortable position as the darlings of American culture if they want to be at the top of their game.

Another consequence of the lion's leadership is often a limited view of creativity. I distinguish two types of creativity, capital C and small *c*. Creativity with a capital C is the kind that leads to breakthrough thinking and new models. Right-brainers tend to thrive on busting old models and creating new ones. They want to move from trains to planes, from bricks-and-mortar to clicks-and-mortar. Left-brainers prefer the subtler form and expressions of creativity—little-*c* creativity—like improving an existing process or tweaking a design . . . perhaps moving from a conventional train to a bullet train. Both forms of creativity are important and valid; to eliminate either is to lose an important tool from the decision kit.

Unfortunately, though, in lion kingdoms that loss is precisely what happens. The following quote is from a lion's description of his team's collaborative process:

> We follow Robert's *Rules of Order*. Each of us present has one vote, and the majority carries . . . . Our client portfolios are nearly identical, which is a natural extension of this focus on one investment philosophy and shared decision making [President and Managing Director, Major Investment Organization].

I purposely omitted this lion's name because he's not presented in a flattering light. This approach to collaborative decision making is not likely to produce wild and crazy new ideas. For starters, just think of the phrase "Robert's *Rules of Order.*" Do the words *rules* and *order* conjure up any notions of breakthrough thinking? Probably not. Henry Martyn Robert was a U.S. general in the 19th century. Does it make sense that a military leader who designed this system more than 100 years ago would create a cutting-edge method for change? No; the rules were designed to manage meetings, control chaos, and maintain or impose order. Different processes, which we'll discuss later, are necessary for opening meetings up to new and radical ideas.

As we discuss lions and their role in the investment world, I think it's fair to ask, "What's wrong with lions as leaders? They have a pretty good success record. Many big firms are thriving. Why change?" True enough. And the premise of this book is not that one style is better than another. Let me repeat that: All styles have value. The danger, though, arises when our thinking becomes limited. Lions may foster an environment that is hostile to creative new ideas.

Where's the evidence for that?

In my work with professional advisors, I've conducted a survey that asks these money managers to rate their organization's culture. On a scale of 1 to 10, they are to rate their organization's culture as far as valuing and encouraging the behaviors in line A or B:

A—Logical thinking, Clarity, Consistency, Idea implementation
B—Creative insights, Flexibility, Risk taking, Idea generation

The many different respondents gave an average rating of 7.5 to line A, and only 5.0 for line B. The significant difference suggests the influence of lions on a firm's culture.

One portfolio manager in Virginia may have put it best. When I asked him what conditions allowed him to produce his most creative work, he said, "When the boss is out of town." It wasn't because he hated his boss—quite the contrary. He liked him. But there was still a different feeling when the boss was gone.

This problem becomes more serious when the lion bosses are under stress. (And who isn't these days?) Myers-Briggs expert Otto Krueger writes, "Striving for efficiency, STJs may produce a work force full of hostility, stress, and absenteeism" (Krueger and Thuesen, *Type Talk at Work*, Tilden Press 1992).

Under stress, we all tend to rely on our tried-and-true, tested strengths. For lions, that means more efficiency and more precision. Do it harder, do it faster. Although this strategy may improve certain aspects of married life, in the work environment it only creates more stress. Which in turn usually results in poorer quality work, poorer results, more stress, and a downward spiral.

But is it really necessary to have all this creativity in the investment field? Isn't the investment world filled with three-piece suits and conservative viewpoints? Where is the evidence that change is needed?

Well, there is no question that it is more difficult to beat the market today. In the 1980s, the rule-of-thumb number was that about a third of professional managers beat the market. In the 1990s, that number dropped to 20 percent, and then down to less than 10 percent. Why is the market getting progressively harder to beat?

One answer is that the market represents the collective wisdom of the investment community, including their tools and information. As investors have become more knowledgeable and better informed, all the while using more powerful tools, the bar has been raised. The importance of higher-quality thinking becomes obvious in this scenario.

But what kind of thinking?

When I started in the investment business in 1979, my first

assignment, as an equity research analyst, was to add a column of numbers. I had an HP calculator and a sheet of figures written in pencil. I added the numbers, got three different answers, took the mean, and gave it to my boss. (He then checked my results and corrected my answer, which left me wondering why he had given me the assignment in the first place.) I progressed in this job to producing spreadsheets of earnings forecasts for various companies—again by hand, with a calculator, erasing the old assumptions and pencilling in the new numbers. In short, I was a glorified computer. I was doing the left-brain, logical number crunching that computers excel at, and for this I was paid reasonably well.

Why is it that computers can beat chess champions like Gary Kasparov and bridge experts like Omar Sharif? Because computers never forget and never make careless mistakes. Therefore, the value of humans with these sorts of left-brained skills is minimal. Computers can now crank out results that are cheap and error-free.

Creative right-brain thinking is different. So far, no computer can match the right brain's capacity to synthesize new information and create new models. The *Wall Street Journal* picked up on this idea in an article entitled, "A New Model for the Nature of Business: It's Alive!" (Feb. 26, 1999). The idea in the article is that a major shift is occurring in thinking about business, away from the mechanistic model to an organic model. Some of the comparisons are shown in Figure 7.2.

What struck me as most significant, though, was the final comparison, labeled "Main economic constraint." It used to be *capital*. Money. Without dough, no business could be successfully launched. The constraint has now become *creativity*. No longer is it necessary to find angels with deep pockets to start new ventures.

An example? Consider Toys 'R' Us and eToys. The former is a huge operation with more than 1,000 stores, 30,000 employees, and $12 billion in revenues. In contrast, eToys is less than a year old at this writing; it has no stores, only 300 employees, and only $100 million in revenues. The kicker? The market places a value

Mechanical Model	Natural Model
Newton	Einstein
Machines	Organisms
Command/Control	Articulate vision
Hierarchies	Self-organizing teams
Land/Energy	Information

Figure 7.2 Business model comparison.

of $4.5 billion on eToys and only $4.0 billion on Toys 'R' Us. eToys
has surpassed the well-established giant, Toys 'R' Us, because of
the former's creativity, not its capital. Thousands of similar examples
exist in today's marketplace. One Arthur Andersen ad attempted
to attract business by pointing this out to corporate leaders:

> Did you hear the one about the guy who decided to take on the
> FORTUNE 500 at home in his spare time?
> (It's not a joke, it's a nightmare.)

Another stated:

> The first thing you have to realize about those wacky kids down
> at new-webco.com is they're not playing by the rules.

Both ads highlight the importance of small startups' using creativity to take a bite out of the corporate leaders' lunch.

What about the experts in the field of investing? Do they see
a need for more creativity?

A recent issue of *Forbes* magazine had no fewer than 12 ads
that emphasized the creativity of the particular firm as its competitive edge. It seems that Madison Avenue, whose job it is to find
what will connect buyers and sellers, has identified innovation as
the critical factor. In fact, experts within the industry also identify
creativity as the key. In a publication by the Association for Investment Management and Research, called *The Future of Investment*

Management (Dec. 1998), editor Katrina Sherrerd sums up the articles in one sentence: "A unifying theme is the need for *innovative strategies* to meet the challenges of the 21st century" (emphasis added).

Another expert in the field, Michael Phillips, President and CEO of Frank Russell Company, writes in the same publication, "Coping with the new trends and the complexities of the business models of today requires *innovative solutions*" (again, emphasis added).

PriceWaterhouseCoopers, a leading name in the consulting field, spent two years researching trends in the investment industry and concluded that the top priority for successful investment firms will be "senior managers who have vision, creativity, flexibility, and a broad perspective" (*Tomorrow's Leading Investment Managers*, PriceWaterhouseCoopers/The Economist Intelligence Unit 1999).

What about customers? Do any studies show that they care about having creative money managers? One study conducted by Dean LeBaron and Gail Farrelly, published in the *Financial Analysts Journal* ("Assessing Risk Tolerance," Jan./Feb. 1989), asked customers to rank the attributes that they would most—and least—like to see in their fund managers. Surprisingly, their two favorites were "creativity" and "willingness to be different." At the other extreme, customers were very negative as to "prizing certainty" and "consensus portfolios." So, yes, customers seem to be supporting the move to more creative money management.

What can be done, then, by individuals or firms?

The Myers-Briggs Type Indicator tool provides direction in this regard. Lots of studies have been conducted to see which Myers-Briggs preferences link up with big-C Creativity (the kind that spawns breakthrough thinking). One study, for example, included 105 professionals from the fields of math, science, architecture, and writing who were rated by their peers as being "highly creative." The participants then took the MBTI assessment instrument. Of the 105, fully 103 showed a preference for iNtuition (N) over Sensing (S).

Another group of tests, conducted by various psychologists, linked personality traits with the Myers-Briggs preferences. The results showed that "sensing-judging" types (lions) were good at finance and creating order. But their counterparts, the "iNtuitive-perceiving" types, excelled at creativity, playfulness, flexibility, autonomy, and (comfort with) complexity.

Still another piece of research, conducted by Gough, established a formula that could be used to rank individuals on the basis of their creativity. The formula is:

$$3SN + JP - EI - .5TF$$

The letters represent the "continuous" score that is generated when one takes the MBTI (i.e., the "long" form of the test). Below are some professions ranked by this formula:

Profession	Score
Architects	366
Playwrights	340
Research scientists	321
Medical school students	276
Engineering students	275
Inventors	258
ISTJ portfolio managers	247
Business executives	221

Note that the STJ (sensing-thinking-judging) portfolio managers ranked in the bottom quarter, along with business execs, indicating a disadvantage if the world is calling for more creative money management. (All studies cited from Myers and McCaulley, *Manual: A Guide to the Development and Use of the Myers-Briggs Type Indicator*, Consulting Psychologist Press 1985). In Chapter 8, we'll look at what can be done by individuals or firms that want to enhance their creativity.

Hang on a minute, though. Okay, so creativity is desirable. But who says we're creatively challenged? Where's the evidence for that statement?

A study presented by Chic Thompson (in a speech entitled, "Being the Change You Seek in the World," Feb. 28, 1996) tallied behaviors of different age groups. On a given day, 44-year-old adults average 11 laughs and 6 questions. On that same day, a 5-year-old will average 113 laughs and 65 questions. Little wonder, then, that a survey on creativity given to the same groups revealed that, of the 5-year-olds, 98 percent had access to their full creative potential—for the 44-year-olds, the number went down to 2 percent! When I ask workshop participants why this happens, I get a list of influences from school regulations ("color within the lines") to critical parents ("don't take risks, just do the right thing") to corporate time constraints ("quit staring out the window and get it done!") to cultural norms ("people won't like you if you're different").

Teresa Amabile, a Harvard professor in innovation, believes that creativity in the workplace gets killed much more often than it gets supported ("How to Kill Creativity," *Harvard Business Review*, Sept./Oct. 1998). She has studied this phenomenon for 20 years and has developed ways to measure if a workplace is creativity-friendly. She summarizes the creativity killers as follows:

- Surveillance and negative judgment by managers and co-workers.
- Lack of freedom (no control over one's own destiny).
- Indifference (lack of support by managers and coworkers).
- Competition (political problems that shut down collaboration between coworkers).
- Time pressures that are externally imposed (and therefore feel stifling).
- Rewards as bribes (if workers feel manipulated by them).

From this evidence, it's pretty obvious that creativity, though certainly not dead, could at least use a jump start.

The remainder of the book is intended to help all of us recovering goodie-two-shoes loosen up and get our creative juices flowing again, especially with regard to investment thinking. How did we lose the inventiveness of those five-year olds? How did we get so realistic, practical, and rigid? In workshops, to help people remember the natural creativity of children, I show clips of young inventors sharing their inventions. The workshop participants laugh out loud at the kids' outrageous creations. It helps to loosen them up for playing with their own ideas.

Try this riddle:

> It is greater than God
> It is more evil than the devil
> Rich people need it
> Poor people have it
> If you eat it you will die.

What is "it?"

After you've thought about it for a minute, consider the following.

When I pose this riddle to workshop participants, I tell them that it was given to a group of kindergarten kids and a group of Stanford MBAs. I then tell them that 80 percent of the kids got the answer, whereas only 17 percent of the MBAs did.

(Oh yes, what is the answer? Nothing. Try it out, you'll see!)

As I'm naturally skeptical, I wasn't sure I believed this research about Stanford MBAs, so I tried it out on a friend's 10-year-old. He was playing a computer game. I settled in beside him and smugly said, "Here's a riddle. It is greater than God." He did not look up from the screen as I spoke, "It is more evil than the devil." As I prepared to say the next part, he interrupted, "Nothing."

"What?" I said, taken aback.

"Nothing," he answered, head down, still playing his game. Amazing. I asked him if he had heard the riddle before, and he shook his head. Remarkable, I thought.

Part Three of this book gives tips on how investors can recover the power of their creative thinking. In the Myers-Briggs framework, this means having full access to the intuitive preference and capabilities. In Carl Jung's language of archetypes, it means accessing the energy of the magician or wizard. Ultimately, it is the capacity to make something of nothing, to take the ordinary and turn it into the extraordinary, to work everyday miracles. For investors, it is the capacity to look at commonly available information and see something different, something significant that will give a competitive edge.

For now, though, let's turn to Part Two, which addresses the state of investment teams today. Using the Myers-Briggs framework, we can analyze the behavior of investment firms and suggest some techniques that might well lead to more success in the markets.

two

The Investment Team: Collaborative Techniques

CHAPTER **8**

Teamwork Today?

Great discoveries and improvements invariably involve the co-operation of many minds. I may be given the credit for having blazed the trail but when I look at the subsequent developments I feel the credit is due to others rather than to myself.
—Alexander Graham Bell

Ideally, teamwork is preferred over solo attempts, with the possible exception of singular talents like Shakespeare or Leonardo da Vinci. There is something unique about that level of genius that suggests collaboration would only dilute the effort. We all know the phrase: "A camel is a horse designed by a committee."

Team training workshops, though, frequently feature an exercise that demonstrates the merits of teamwork. Typically the exercise involves a shipwreck on an uninhabited island or a plane crash in the desert. The participants first plan their rescue alone, picking items that they think they'll need from a master list. Then they pool their intellectual talents and try to solve the rescue problem together. Invariably the team does better than any one individual alone, thereby proving once and for all that we should all avoid sailing or flying. Whoops, wrong conclusion. The correct conclusion from the team exercise is that teamwork provides better solutions than working alone.

Is this true for investment decision making? Should we join investment clubs? Should professionals work in teams? Do the masters that we've been studying work in teams?

Let's start with the masters. The answer for them is a paradox. (By now you realize that most of my suggestions are paradoxical. I believe that is the nature of the world we live in: the great truths are the ones where the opposite of a truth is true as well.) The masters are lone wolves who love their independence. They are also collaborators who rely completely on the help of trusted colleagues. Buffett, for example, makes fun of meetings and quips about the best meetings being the ones where he talks to himself in the mirror. And yet he works hand-in-glove with Charlie Munger. He trusts Munger's judgment and runs ideas past him constantly. That's why Buffett claims that the two of them can craft a four-page letter with three grunts on the phone.

Zweig has a similar relationship with Joe DiMenna. In fact, their relationship fits well with the model that we've been discussing: integrating different personality styles to be more effective in thinking. Zweig says that DiMenna is the better of the two at poring over financial statements and getting all the details. So, they specialize and leverage their talents.

If the masters benefit from collaborating, how about professional investors in general? What is the state of teamwork in the profession? Interestingly, one of the hottest funds right now is the Janus Fund. That's an apt name for teamwork in the investment field; Janus is the Roman god with two faces. Similarly, there is much lip service from investment leaders about the importance of teamwork. For example, Gary Brinson of Brinson Partners says that "almost out of necessity, we need to collaborate and work together to achieve the objectives that we all want to achieve" (*Managing Investment Firms: People and Culture*, AIMR Publications 1996).

Another major figure in the field, David Fisher, Chairman of the Board at the Capital Group of Companies, Inc., says, "The most important lesson I have learned is never to forget that invest-ment management is a people business" (*Managing Investment Firms: People and Culture*, AIMR Publications 1996).

Yet another leader in the field, James Rothenberg, President of Capital Research, says that there are two models in the investment profession: the star model (depends on a few stars, like Michael Jordan in basketball) and the team model (depends on collabora-tion). In Rothenberg's words, "Capital has very few stars that anyone would recognize. Only one or two individuals get much press coverage, which is all part of our effort to promote team-work and cooperation" (*Managing Investment Firms: People and Culture*, AIMR Publications 1996).

Investment companies make the same claims in full-page ads. One Group Mutual Funds touts its "Solid Performance built on Discipline, Consistency, and Teamwork." Another leading firm, Franklin Mutual Series Fund, boasts that their "team's activist approach has proven itself through market upswings and down-swings."

One of the trends in the investment business is hiring entire teams rather than one high-profile individual. A recent *Wall Street Journal* headline read: "Teams of Fund Managers Jumping Ship." The article noted that "[i]n recent months, Merrill Lynch & Co. lifted a 12-person group of indexing specialists from Deutsche Bank AG, which turned around and nabbed eight officials from State Street Global Advisors" (Oct. 15, 1999).

The major firms are using a portfolio concept—diversification—in the management of their people. Instead of putting all the eggs in one basket, and depending on a Peter-Lynch-like star, the firms are hiring teams; if one individual leaves, the remaining team can still boast a good record with an "intact" team. This strategy of plucking entire teams away from competitors is a reaction to the team approach.

All of this emphasis on teams is fine, but it may not reflect reality Putting four people in a room and saying, "Okay, you're now a team" has no more significance than handing four people musical scores and saying, "You are now a barbershop quartet." Teams depend on leadership, processes, experience, agreements, and trust. They don't just happen, any more than functional families just happen. This is particularly interesting when you remember that Patrick O'Donnell from Putnam (mentioned at the outset of this book) says that the investment business "has a critical shortage of people who enjoy managing people." In O'Donnell's effort to fill that gap and become more expert in managing investment professionals, he turned to the research in the field—and found that it is virtually nonexistent. Even the few leaders, like O'Donnell, who *do* enjoy managing people have had to create their own processes and tools. (O'Donnell calls it "nurturing" and makes no apology for a male in the investment business relating to his team members in this way.) Doesn't this dearth of information seem odd in an industry that is full of people touting the benefits of teamwork? That's why I suspect much of the ado about teamwork consists of lip service and buzzwords; there's little evidence of any serious involvement.

Another oddity? A company called Interaction Associates (IA), masters at training teams from all industries to work collaboratively, has no money management teams as clients. IA has been working with many of the leading investment firms: Fidelity, Morgan Stanley, Oppenheimer, and others. The clients have been delighted with the results, which have involved various teams from around the company, but—importantly—no money managers. What invisible force is keeping collaborative skills training away from the money managers? If we're to believe the people quoted earlier, money managers are all giddy for teamwork.

Here is another piece of evidence from personal experience. My colleague, Brian Muldoon (author of *The Heart of Conflict*, Putnam 1996), and I conducted a workshop in Chicago on the topic of creative collaboration for investment professionals. The promotional material was sent to 1,700 practicing investment professionals in this area. In response, 12 brave pioneers signed up. The participant feedback was as follows:

> "The learnings were uniquely rich; the strong quantitative skills of the IASC attendees were challenged and complemented by the layering of qualitative skills necessary for creativity and collaboration. My expectations were greatly surpassed. Effective teaching methods that encourage immediate application of learnings to real work/life situations."
>
> "Terrific workshop. Good practical skills for investment teams."
>
> "Day flew by—excellent involvement (not too much, not too little). Many interesting exercises to take back to the office."
>
> "Quality of instruction and content was excellent."

When we reviewed this feedback, obviously we were pleased. We did what any red-blooded American marketer would do: we printed up a course description with these endorsements—from satisfied customers of the new product—and sent it out again to the 1,700 local members. Further, we sent the promotional material to more than 50 local investment chapters (comprised of 37,000 CFA designation holders worldwide) around the country, which could have translated into several thousand more prospects.

Given the preceding discussion about the importance of teamwork in the investment field, you might think that this sort of training, designed by and for investment professionals, would be a smash hit. Brian and I expected to have to free our schedules for weeks to come to handle the deluge of requests, especially after it was "tested" (first set of guinea pigs had attended) and became a proven product.

The results? Three people signed up locally, and three chapter presidents called with lukewarm inquiries. That was it. The local workshop was cancelled because of low turnout, and none of the inquiries from around the country resulted in additional training bookings.

The purpose of my reporting this is not to portray ourselves as pathetic (like the lonely Maytag repairmen of the investment industry). Rather, the point is to highlight the paradox of an industry that is beating a large drum and shouting, "We believe in teamwork" while demonstrating no real interest in learning the skills.

I finally got so curious about this phenomenon that I contacted nearly 50 friends in the industry nationwide and simply asked, "Do you know of any money managers that have done team training?" I have received many responses, but not one lead yet.

Well, maybe investment teams already know the skills. Maybe they don't need the training. Possibly. Certainly at some firms this is true. But my experience, and that of Patrick O'Donnell, Interaction Associates, and others, tends to argue against that position for the general industry. O'Donnell states that:

> The investment management industry is only now beginning to focus on the challenge of managing itself. Morningstar recently updated the employee turnover numbers for the top 20 mutual fund companies. These numbers are startling. A few companies have no turnover in some years; others have double-digit employee turnover in a single year or maybe for two years in a row ["The Future of Investment Management," AIMR Publications, Dec. 1998].

Teams, like friendships and marriages, need careful attention so that trust and respect can develop. It's impossible to boast of good teamwork when members are coming and going at a high rate.

The issue of trust brings to mind another experience of mine working with investment professionals. I was working with a major investment firm to deliver a workshop in diversity. The business case for the course was the benefits of leveraging differences: cultural, gender, thinking styles, and so on. The logic was that people would work better if there were an inclusive, trusting, cooperative environment. The company in question used a survey to determine the attitudes of department members on these matters. Statements to be evaluated included: "I am treated with respect and dignity," and "The environment fosters a sense of trust and openness." Respondents ranked these statements, as applied to their situations, using a spectrum from "definitely no" to "definitely yes."

The workshop was mandatory and participants (professional investors) were resistant, to say the least. I'm sure half of them would rather have had root canals performed without anesthesia than be in an experiential "touchy-feely" workshop. The body language and general chill in the classroom on the first morning did not bode well. Furthermore, my cotrainer and I had not delivered this version of the workshop before, so this was our maiden voyage. (Actually, my cotrainer, a woman, had never delivered any workshops before.) The investment professionals in the room, mostly thinking types as we've discussed earlier, turned their analytic abilities up to "high" and posed every possible objection as to why this class was a complete and utter waste. By the second day, I had already dubbed this the Chernobyl of training experiences.

Toward the close of the workshop, in an effort to turn the mood more positive, I asked the group, "Well, what *can* you say that is positive about this experience?" Frank, an attorney in the investment department, raised his hand and said, "I knew all this material already, so I think this has been a huge waste of my time." (At this point, my cotrainer—the smart one—left the room in tears. I remained in the room and did my version of Mohammed Ali's "rope-a-dope.")

The only positive learning from the day came at the very end, when I told this group that the workshop was over. I got a new appreciation for the time interval of a nanosecond, because the room emptied in one.

The story has an interesting epilogue, though. The survey I

mentioned indicated that this group of investors had the lowest scores in the entire company on the questions concerning trust, respect, and openness. Apparently, the very people who needed these skills the most had no interest in them. Puzzling as this may seem, the *New York Times* article about overconfidence (cited in Chapter 5) seems to explain it: we don't know what we don't know. The people who talk too much don't realize it, the people who tell humorless jokes, the people who write boring investment books . . . oops. The reason for this might appear mysterious at first, but the explanation is really pretty simple. To judge our performance accurately, we would have to know what it means to perform badly. Most investment teams that I've worked with are comprised of talented, bright, ambitious people who are clueless about teamwork. Typically their bosses, who should teach and coach them, don't know either. Why? They got to be bosses by doing their technical jobs well. One chief investment officer of a major firm told me that if he had to choose between a technical expert and a good generalist to run a department, he would take the technical expert. That firm has been in disarray for years, with high turnover, low morale, and shrinking assets. Is it any wonder?

What can investment firms do to stimulate creative collaboration in their money management teams? We'll examine that question in later chapters, but first Chapter 9 has another reason why investment organizations tend to be poor environments for teamwork.

Golden Gloves or Golden Rule?

Real learning comes about when the competitive spirit has ceased.
—J. Krishnamurti

There is another reason why creative collaboration is difficult to achieve in investment firms. As thinking (T) types, investors tend to be very competitive. They like a good fight. They see the world as win-lose, rather than win-win. The consequences of investors' preference for thinking is highlighted each time Brian and I facilitate an exercise called the "Prisoner's Dilemma." This game explores the way in which individuals interact. Do they tend to be trusting and cooperative, or are they cautious and competitive?

The Prisoner's Dilemma was originally formulated by mathematician Albert W. Tucker in the 1950s and has since become the classic example of a non-zero-sum game. (A *zero-sum game* is simply a win-lose game, such as chess. For each winner, there's a loser. If I win, you lose. A non-zero-sum game allows cooperation. There are moves that benefit both players, and this is what makes these games interesting.) In the Prisoner's Dilemma, two suspects are picked up by the police and interrogated in separate cells without a chance to communicate with each other. For the purpose of this game, it makes no difference whether the suspects actually committed the crime. They are both told the same thing:

If you both snitch on each other, you will both get three years in prison.

If neither of you snitches, the police will have no evidence and you will both go free.

If one of you snitches but the other doesn't, the snitcher will make a deal with the police and will go free while the other one goes to jail for six years.

At first glance the correct strategy appears obvious. No matter what the other suspect does, you'll be better off informing ("snitching"). Maddeningly, the other suspect realizes this as well, so you both end up getting three years. Ironically, if you had both "cooperated" (refused to snitch), you would both be much better off.

The goal is to figure out the other suspect's strategy and use it to reduce your total jail time. The other suspect will be doing the same.

The movie *L.A. Confidential* contains a classic scene of the Prisoner's Dilemma. About 55 minutes into the film, Lt. Ecksley conducts an interrogation of three suspects in the Night Owl Massacre. He places them in three different rooms, with one-way mirrors and sound equipment so that the other suspects can hear the person that Ecksley is questioning. At one point, Ecksley exactly poses the Prisoner's Dilemma, when he says to the second suspect, "Ray Collins just ratted you off. He said that the Night Owl was your idea. I think it was Ray's idea. If you talk I think I can save your life. Son, six people are dead. Someone has to pay for that. Now, it can be you or it can be Ray." By playing both sides against the middle, Ecksley gets the suspect to confess.

In our classroom exercise, we use blue and red chips to symbolize "snitch" and "cooperate." Each team confers and then places a chip in an envelope and passes it to the facilitators. The scoring, following the options described earlier, is shown in Figure 9.1.

The scores are posted and another round is played. After the second round, teams are allowed to negotiate based on the chips played so far. The winning team at the end has the highest posi-

	Red Scores	Blue Scores
All play red	+3	—
All play blue	—	–3
Some play red, some play blue	–6	+6

Figure 9.1   Scoring of the Prisoner's Dilemma.

tive score. If no team has a positive score, the facilitators keep the prizes.

We have played the game with a wide range of groups, from nonprofit to for-profit organizations, from lawyers to healthcare professionals to the fiercest lions on Wall Street. The results, as you can imagine, are very different. The healthcare workers started the game with a mix: some cooperating, some competing. After a while the group created a vision, shared among all the teams, that they would give the prize money to United Way! This vision united the group. They cooperated from that point on, won the prize money, and gave it to charity.

The scenario was a bit different when we played this game with professional investors at a financial analysts' seminar at Northwestern University. From the outset, it was war, with the exception of one poor team that tried to wave the white flag and was buried, never to recover for the rest of the game. The other teams battled it out, tooth and nail, cutting deals, forming alliances and then breaking them. Machiavelli would have burst his buttons. The final round of the game found two teams tied for the lead. Sure enough, one co-leader cut a deal with a losing team that allowed them to share the winnings. Several observations resulted from watching investors play the game:

- Most of the participants delighted in the competition.
- No other group has ever approached that level of deal making.

- The motivation of revenge explained the collaboration by the two teams in the final round. (They had been betrayed by the third team and were delighted to repay it in kind. Clearly, an eye-for-an-eye strategy was at work.)

On a different occasion, we took a group of financial executives and divided them by their thinking and feeling preferences. About two-thirds of the finance department had a preference for thinking (nearly all the professionals); the other third (mostly the support staff) had a preference for feeling. We played the Prisoner's Dilemma with the thinking team versus the feeling team. True to form, the thinkers were competitive, whereas the feelers employed a cooperative strategy. As the rounds were played, the feelers fell farther behind in the score and began to voice their anger about the thinkers' style of play. The conflict came to a head in the last round, and, during negotiation, the thinkers finally agreed to cooperate—to go for the win-win solution. The teams separated for their last declaration of "blue" or "red." To the utter astonishment of the feelers, the thinkers violated the agreement and chose to compete! At that point, the room went semi-ballistic. There was general chaos, with outbursts and name-calling. When we finally got the group quieted, the feelers insisted on knowing why the thinkers had broken their promise.

The response from the captain of the thinking team was simple: "Hey, it was only a game. We were playing to win." That rationale made perfect sense to the thinkers and almost none to the feelers. (For weeks afterward, department morale was shaky at best. Brian and I thought of changing our slogan to "Team Morale: you build it, we crush it!") The ability of thinkers to be objective and factual makes them excellent analysts and decision makers, but these same attributes are liabilities when it comes to forming teams and maintaining good relations.

Whether it takes the form of an investment club or a formal group of investment professionals, would teamwork help in the investment process? The evidence from the group I spoke of earlier, the five-person team, suggests that it would. Would a cooperative environment stimulate creativity? Evidence from Alfie Kohn suggests that it would. In his book, *No Contest: The Case Against Competition* (Houghton Mifflin 1992), he shows that when internal competition was encouraged within a company, it resulted in less creative work.

Is the investment industry moving toward more teamwork? I don't see much evidence of it, despite all the advertising puffery. The investment industry still operates on the model of stars—talented virtuosos who rely on their own genius to collect, assimilate, and process information and decide which investments to make.

Chapter 10 suggests a different, more powerful way for teams to collaborate, based on the strengths of different personality styles.

Tools for Investment Teams

Be really whole and all things will come to you.
—Lao Tzu

Many years ago, in a conference room on the 16th floor of the First Chicago Bank building, Gary Brinson, the new chief investment officer, said to his staff: "Investment people tend to be good at one of three things. Either they are good at collecting the data, or they are good at analyzing it, or they are good at taking the analysis and making some decisions to implement." Brinson's theory of the specialization of labor must have impressed me—obviously, if I've remembered it for all these years—and makes perfect sense given Myers-Briggs as a backdrop. The talents of an investment team, or any team, can be employed most effectively by conscious attention to the team members' preferences and how they use them in a group decision-making process.

Experts in collaboration skills understand and teach this principle. For example, Interaction Associates uses an exercise called "Planning a Vacation" in training classes. Participants are asked to consider how they plan vacations and which steps they take first. The choices include:

- Collecting data about destinations, cost, availability, and the like.
- Imagining the perfect vacation.
- Packing and going.
- Weighing different alternatives and then choosing one.

Once participants choose the order in which they would do these activities, they are then asked to stand with others who had the same first choice. Four groups form. The discussion that follows explores ways in which groups can work most effectively, given their different approaches to problem solving.

IDENTIFYING PREFERENCES

When looked at through the lens of Myers-Briggs, in the vacation exercise the participants are subtly being asked to identify their preferences. The data collectors have a preference for sensing (S). The imaginers have a preference for iNtuition (N). The pack-and-go types are more action-oriented feelers (F). The weighers of alternatives are thinking (T) types. The point of the exercise is to clearly show the participants that people go about making decisions differently. Lots of time and energy are wasted in meetings because all these different approaches are being tried simultaneously. A better starting place is to acknowledge the different approaches and then reach agreement on a plan of attack.

My old boss Brinson, though he didn't know it explicitly, was pointing out that some analysts are sensing types: really good at digging out the data. That is their contribution. An example of such an analyst is James Chanos. He made his reputation by digging deeper into the facts than any other analysts were willing to go. Indeed, an article in the *Wall Street Journal* said, "Young Analyst Defied 'Experts' and Foresaw Baldwin United's Ills." The article praised Chanos for his detail-oriented approach: "Mr. Chanos started poring over piles of Baldwin's financial statements . . . . The key to spotting that pattern lay in obscure reports that Baldwin was required to file with the state insurance regulators, and Mr. Chanos obtained the reports at the suggestion of Ray Dirks" (Darling, "Picking a Loser," *Wall Street Journal*, Sept. 28, 1983).

The second type of analyst that Brinson described is intuitive, with the capacity to take the facts and spot unusual patterns. We marvel at Sherlock Holmes when he solves a case with his incredible intellect. Invariably he chides Watson, "You see but you do not observe." He means, of course, that all of us see the same material, read the same papers, and listen to same news reports—but some of us (like Holmes) are able to see a different pattern. In fact, Holmes says of himself that his talent is the unusual interplay of imagination and reality in his reasoning. Well, that's what we've been discussing. An analyst like Chanos is great at finding the reality, the deep reality behind the numbers. An intuitive analyst, with Holmes-like intuition, can take those facts and discern patterns that others cannot see.

An example of an intuitive investor is Dean LeBaron, formerly of Batterymarch. I remember attending a management meeting with Intel in which LeBaron was sitting in the back, quietly taking notes. Various analysts were peppering management with questions, all aimed at exposing the mother lode of hidden value or sham. There was a pause for just a moment, and then LeBaron lobbed his question from the back of the room. To this day I can't remember what the question was—I wish I could. What I do remember was a sea of blank analyst faces, with their heads cocked like listening dogs, all clueless as to what LeBaron was talking about. All except the chief financial officer of Intel. He looked toward the back of the room and smiled, his face seeming to say, "So, one of you has seen beyond the smoke and mirrors to the real issue." He gave a short answer; LeBaron wrote it down and then promptly left the room. The rest of us knew that something had happened, that a buy or sell signal had been revealed, but none of us knew which.

LeBaron, a highly intuitive, creative investor, had discerned a pattern underlying all the data.

Brinson's third investor is the thinker (T) and judger (J). This person is action-oriented and quick to move on an idea. Typically such people don't complicate their world with lots of different possibilities. They "keep it simple, stupid." They know what has worked for them and, like Zweig and his hero Livermore, they stick to the rules. Their discipline is often what allows them to win and to endure tough markets.

The question, though, is how these different personality talents can come together on a team. How does one harness their distinctive abilities? The way to get teams to work well together has two aspects: (1) conscious attention to the different styles and (2) a process for working with those styles. The different styles and their strengths and weaknesses have already been addressed, so let's turn to the process for working as a team.

GETTING A TEAM WORKING TOGETHER

Good chemistry matters. In my experience, team leaders are better off picking members among whom there is good rapport, which means trust and respect and positive intention—basically, the mutual desire to achieve a clearly stated goal. Although this may sound obvious, too many teams start off with poor personal relations (or even an out-and-out saboteur) and try to work through those headaches. Some experts say that these headaches are inevitable. Forming, storming, norming, and performing is natural law and will happen with any group. To some extent that's true. All teams experience some friction. But the leader has to determine what is healthy conflict and what is destructive to the team's momentum. Again, knowledge of personality types is essential for these judgment calls. Otherwise, a "judging" team captain may toss out the "perceiving" participants because they drag out the discussions and never want to reach closure. Though annoying to the judging types, this dynamic can be healthy and stimulate good decision making. The goal is to create an environment characterized by what O'Donnell calls "creative conflict." He writes:

> The problem with conflict is that it can easily be mistaken for strife. Creative conflict is a facilitator of good decision making, but strife is cognitively distressing, which lowers the odds that thinking will be accurate. Conflict focuses on issues; strife, on personalities, whether overtly or sub rosa. The manager needs to be comfortable with conflict and willing to let it continue without trying to bring it to a premature resolution [*Managing Investment Firms: People and Culture*, AIMR Publications 1996].

Again, the "judging" team leader may want to do just that: reach resolution too quickly. Similarly, the "feeling" team captain may be uncomfortable with any conflict, given a preference for harmony and friendship. Orchestrating this team conflict constructively is the leader's job, and knowledge of personality styles is helpful.

Consider the three critical elements of investment decision making that were identified in Brinson's remark: gathering details (sensing), analyzing (intuition), and deciding (thinking). Recognizing, understanding, and leveraging these talents in a meeting is very powerful. In a typical investment meeting, the conversation will start in one of two places, usually referred to as "top-down" or "bottom-up." The top-down approach starts with the big picture: the economy, interest rates, world markets, exchange rates, major news headlines. Investors with a preference for intuition thrive in this environment. They like talking about concepts and patterns and trading what-if scenarios. The sensors will get bored quickly. To them, theory is useless without good, hard facts.

The sensors would prefer to start the discussion from the bottom up. Let's begin with some company information, some actual holdings, winning and losing stocks, portfolio performance. They will give lots of details about holdings, with complete backup in the form of numbers and graphs. The intuitives will now be glazing over. They find details—without a theory or pattern behind the mass of data—uninteresting.

So how do the preferences get reconciled? First, acknowledge that both styles of thought are valid, and then decide how to integrate them for best results. The process that I've used with teams is to designate the preferences as "filters." Consider them as eyeglasses through which we see the world. The sensing (S) types wear filters that allow them to focus on details. The intuitives (N) have glasses that help them pick out patterns and see beyond the surface information. Thinkers (T) have filters that help them see objectively. Feelers (F) use filters that allow them to see how people are reacting to the decisions. In my workshops, the filters are assigned colors (see Figure 10.1).

Participants are encouraged to choose the order in which the filters will be used, and to be conscious of which filter they are using. To get an idea of why this process is effective, imagine the first assembly lines. Instead of having assembly people work independently, Henry Ford thought that productivity could be enhanced by having them specialize in one area. The assembly line was created and mass production was born. Similarly, when individuals in a meeting use one filter at a time, they avoid the inefficiency of having several different conversations occurring simultaneously.

Obvious as it may seem, this mistake occurs all the time in meetings, even at the highest levels. One large insurance firm was putting a major effort (time and money) into redefining its customer experience. I was facilitating some of the brainstorming

Blue	Sensing (S): facts, details	Blue police uniforms: facts
Yellow	Intuitive (N): creativity	Yellow light bulb: ideas
Green	Thinking (T): evaluating	Green money: bottom-line
Red	Feeling (F): activating	Red passion: heart and blood

Figure 10.1   Color assignments for thought-style preference "filters."

meetings. Twenty senior executives from the home office sat around a conference table. A pattern emerged almost as soon as the discussion began. The senior marketing executive would offer a new idea and immediately the controller would evaluate and discard it. Every time an idea was buried, it was for one of the six classic reasons:

1. It will never work.
2. We can't afford it.
3. We've never done it that way before.
4. We're not ready for it.
5. It's not our responsibility.
6. We're doing fine without it.

I had assumed that at this senior level, the tools for creative collaboration were known and practiced. Not so! The right-brained creators and the left-brained evaluators were doing what they normally do, wrestling and struggling. Tempers began to flare, people took things personally, frustration mounted, and heels dug in deeper. This is the first danger of "unconscious" meetings: People with the best of intentions can end up at war with one another because they don't understand the use of filters. I stopped the group and told them the story about the fellow moving his piano:

> A man is moving his piano. It's half in and half out of his apartment. He struggles and struggles and works and works. Finally, a neighbor walks by and offers to help. The owner sighs and says, "Great." The two of them struggle for half an hour without any gain. Finally the owner says, "It's no use; we'll never get it out!" At which point the neighbor says, "Out?"

The point of the story is simple: Coordinated effort is necessary for results. If the insurance group had continued in its original fashion, both groups would have been exhausted and frustrated by the end of the meeting, and very little would have been accomplished.

Blue	Yellow	Green	Red
Details	Creativity	Benefits	Gut reactions
Figures	Alternatives	Advantages	Feelings
Data	Possibilities	Costs	Attitudes
Information needed	New ideas	Concerns	Impressions

Figure 10.2   Words associated with different filter (personality) types.

Probably, as an intervention, the leader in the room would have taken over and steered the decision making (consciously or not) in a direction that he liked. To say the least, this does not produce the best collaborative results.

The process for improving investment decision making, then, is to recognize the different personality styles and develop some skill in using the filters during discussions. As an aid in this skill development, Figure 10.2 lists some typical words associated with the different filters. Teams that really want to learn the skills should consider the kind of training that Interaction Associates and other organizations offer.

Perhaps investment organizations will get serious about the benefits of collaborative action in the future, but for now it seems clear that they are achieving enough success with a disguised star system. For those of you who still question this statement, count the number of ads that feature one investment professional (Lynch, Buffett, etc.) and the number of those that picture a team. It's still mostly a lone-wolf industry, with the spotlights on a few brilliant gurus dispensing their financial wisdom.

"Okay," you say. "This sounds promising, but are there any management teams using these tools currently?"

Yes, and we'll cover that next in Chapter 11.

Case History

Collaboration for a Money Management Team

Coming together is a beginning; keeping together is progress; working together is success.

—Henry Ford

The team that I worked with consists of five people, all professional money managers, running about $2.5 billion of common-stock money. In a radical departure from traditional approaches to money management, all the members agreed to operate as a team, including consensus decision making. Further, their reward for beating the benchmark S&P 500 was lumped together so that they were truly aligned with the goal. As the Three Musketeers used to say, "All for one, and one for all." If they don't beat the benchmark, none of them gets a bonus, including the leader.

Their main objective in operating as a team was to harness the power of their collective thinking, especially the creativity. Accordingly, four of the members of the team have a preference for intuition (N), whereas only one prefers sensing (S). See Figure 11.1 for the compositional breakdown. The sensing teammate provides a good grounding when the big-picture boys get too far off into dreamland.

Team Members		Left Brain				Right Brain	
Name	Type	Sensing	Thinking	Judging	Intuitive	Feeling	Perceiving
Dave	NTJ		X	X	X		
Jeff	NTJ		X	X	X		
Peter	NTP		X		X		X
Bob	NFP				X	X	X
Paul	STJ	X	X	X			
Totals		1	4	3	4	1	2

Left brain = 8   Right brain = 7

Figure 11.1   Team composition by types.

As with the thinking function, four of the team members have a preference for thinking, with only one having a feeling preference. As indicated earlier, most investment professionals are thinkers. The advantage of having a feeler is that quite often that person is the glue that holds the team together and smoothes over the rough spots. Feelers are natural-born peacemakers. (It's said that Paul McCartney—a feeler—was the glue that held the Beatles together through all their interpersonal battles.) The feeler on this investment team is no exception. Quick to joke and smile, he lightens up the atmosphere and provides a friendly presence. Thinkers tend to like locking horns and debating. They often look for win-lose outcomes. It's useful to have a team member who is naturally looking for win-wins.

The other two scales—Extraverted versus Introverted (not shown) and Organized (Js) versus Flexible (Ps)—are evenly balanced on this team. Importantly, the presence of two Flexible types (Perceivers) on the team helps keep the creativity level high. Perceivers are natural "openers." They like to ask more and more questions and put additional options on the table. The tension pulling them in the other direction—the balancer—is the judger, who likes to close the discussion and settle on a plan. It's useful to have a judger as the team leader, which in fact this team does. His inclination is to make a decision and move, which in the case of investing is often more important than taking extra time to mull over ideas.

The description of this team may sound ideal. All hearts and flowers, perfect harmony. Not so. Along the way, the leader has had to make some tough choices. To get the chemistry he wanted, he had to replace two people. One person was ultimately dropped because she had too much of a lion approach to thinking and teamwork. She tended to resist any new ideas, finding fault with them immediately and arguing that the old, tried-and-true ways work best. Eventually, the team leader removed her because the rest of the team felt inhibited bringing up unusual, radical ideas.

Because this team was planned to foster dynamic tension—in other words, it was constructed to have each of the preferences represented—there will never be a resting point for the team. The leader's job is to continuously monitor the tension in the group, sometimes encouraging more debate when things go flat, and at other times reining it in. The image is that of a guitar, which can produce beautiful music only if the strings are appropriately tight. Too tight, they snap. Too loose, they don't produce a pitch. The leader on this team has a difficult job, daily watching the dynamics of this group.

The results so far? In 1999 the team's portfolio returned 25.13 percent, as opposed to the S&P 500 (less tobacco and liquor) 22.48 percent. They outperformed by 265 basis points. Not bad for the first year, especially given the very conservative risk posture, and a tracking error of less than 2 percent.

Of course, one year means very little, but there is a side benefit that isn't measured in the portfolio results. The team is committed to having fun as well as outperforming the S&P. With this as a goal, they win regardless of the numbers. As Warren Buffett says, "I tap-dance into work each day."

This idea of diversifying the talent to get a more creative environment is catching on with other financial concerns. Two major banks have added the intuitive preference to their senior manager level. At Sovran Bank, for example, management used the MBTI to add the visionary element to the senior team. Consultant R. Steven Terrell, who worked with Sovran's management, said that Sovran "has attempted to integrate strategic, visionary leadership with traditional, conservative bank management practices." He also noted that "[k]nowledge about type distribution at Sovran has proven to be very useful." Figure 11.2 details Sovran's conscious choice to add more intuitive-creative types at the highest level of the corporation.

Likewise, a major bank in South Africa used a similar strategy, with the result that three-quarters of its senior management has a

Level	Number	NF	NT	SJ	SP
Nonexempt	247	14%	14%	59%	13%
Exempt	377	11	30	44	15
Senior	80	6	36	50	8
Executive	10	0	60	40	0

Figure 11.2 Personality types preference distribution at Sovran Bank.

preference for intuition (see Figure 11.3). The danger there, as you can guess, is that they generate lots of wonderful ideas, many of which are impractical or hard to implement. Again, the recurring theme in all of this diversification is *balance*. The strings of the instrument must be just tight enough to hit the perfect pitch.

These examples compellingly show that the Myers-Briggs diagnostic tool can help determine how to get more creativity out of yourself or your team.

Individuals with a preference for intuition (N) have an edge in the creative department, but those with a preference for sensing (S) can still take steps to add big-C Creativity to their investment portfolio. Without this "N" factor in their thinking, investors are likely to become limited in their viewpoint and miss the next curve in the road. There are plenty of examples from history of intelligent people making "dumb" statements because they could not see the changes coming. A few of the more famous ones:

Level	Number	NF	NT	SJ	SP
Exempt	44	5%	27%	55%	14%
Senior	24	8	33	50	8
Executive	16	0	75	13	2

Figure 11.3 Personality type preference distribution at a South African bank.

"Heavier-than-air flying machines are impossible." (Lord Kelvin, 1895)

"Everything that can be invented has been invented." (Charles Duells, Patent Office director, 1899)

"It is an idle dream to imagine that . . . automobiles will take the place of railways in the long distance movement of people." (American Railroad Congress, 1913)

"There is no likelihood that man can ever tap the power of the atom." (Robert Millikan, Nobel prizewinner in physics, 1920)

"Who the hell wants to hear actors talk?" (Harry Warner, 1927)

"There is no reason for any individual to have a computer in their home." (Ken Olson, president of Digital Equipment Corporation, 1977)

"The Beatles will go nowhere." (Decca Records, 1963)

The investment profession is not immune to the same sorts of laughable mistakes. Here are some beauties:

"Bonds will outperform stocks." (Typical 1920s investor)

"Diversification is undesireable. One or two, or at most three or four securities should be bought." (Gerald Loeb, 1950)

"We believe that growth stocks are the soundest and safest plan for the average investor." (T. Rowe Price, 1960)

"The stock market is efficient." (Jim Ware, student at University of Chicago, 1978).

As you can see, no one is exempt from the making of dumb statements.

One major bank is currently running ads that feature serious-looking career people saying things like, "Our job is to see around corners." Uh-huh. The people pictured are wearing the most conservative outfits that big money can buy . . . and they are supposed to be the wild and crazy types who dream up the next zany idea.

Well, maybe. My guess is that the freaky-looking guys with pony-tails, tattoos, and various pierced body parts (like Stuart, the Ameritrade online trader on TV) will be the major innovators. You won't dig up too many photos of Bill Gates wearing a pin-striped suit and suspenders.

So, how does one stretch one's creative ability? First off, the exercises mentioned in Chapter 5 will help sensing types stretch into their big "C."

Perhaps a more practical approach is to diversify one's own personality talent in the same way that fund managers diversify their portfolios. Diversification is known to be a powerful positive force in investing. Simply put, diversification means avoiding the mistake of putting all your eggs in one basket. One relatively simple solution to more creativity is to embrace diversity. Ameritrade's TV ad with freaky Stuart and his older, conservative boss is a perfect example: the conservative "lion" teaming up with the wild "jester." There is already evidence in the markets that diversity works. The Fortune Diversity Fund, which includes companies that have the highest marks for diversity, is an example. Their stocks did better than the S&P 500 Index. Partly this is because diversity adds more firepower to the quality of thinking. This kind of diversity can be consciously added to investment clubs or money management teams.

Having discussed the nature of collaboration in the investment arena, and looked at some suggestions for improvement, I want to shift our focus to personality temperaments. How do they affect the markets? How do they affect client service?

CHAPTER 12

Temperaments and Teams

Implications for the Markets

Hippocrates gave us the first fourfold analogy of human differences to call our attention to four distinct patterns of habitual behavior.

—David Keirsey, author of *Portraits of Temperament*

At the outset of this book, I mentioned that the market is getting smarter. How? Imagine the stock market as being like the Borg from the Star Trek series. The Borg are an alien race that is part machine and part organic. They travel through space in a huge, sinister black cube assimilating other civilizations and species into what they call their "collective." Their goal is to assimilate all races. The secret of the Borg's success is that all the individual Borg units are connected to one another; essentially, they have a hive mind. They share thoughts instantly, so their learning curve is instantaneous. As soon as one of them learns something important, the rest of them know it. Hence, in battle they are able to analyze an enemy's weapons and immediately reconfigure themselves into an invincible force. When members of the Federation (the good guys) shoot Borg units with phasers, they can vaporize only a few Borg before the rest of the Borg become immune to the blast. Consequently, the Federation, as in a game of chess, has to think several steps ahead of the Borg to defeat them.

In the markets we face today, as soon as winning strategies are identified, the market "morphs" to absorb them and render them ineffective. Winning strategies have to be designed to stay a step ahead, continually reinventing the next version of the strategy. It seems that almost all information is available instantaneously now. On the Internet, for example, you can find out not only how many trees are growing in North Dakota, but also how many red-headed woodpeckers are living on each one of them. The Internet represents a huge collective consciousness. And guess what? You are up against that giant brain. Now, I ask that old geezer in the print ad—the one saying, "9,763 stocks. I like my odds.": Do you still like your odds?

But there is still another way in which the market is changing that makes it harder to predict and, therefore, to win. This second way involves the personality styles that we've been discussing. The mix is changing.

Let me use John Maynard Keynes's beauty contest analogy to explain how:

> [P]rofessional investment may be likened to those newspaper competitions in which the competitors have to pick out the six prettiest faces from a hundred photographs, the prize being awarded to the competitor whose choice most nearly corresponds to the average preferences of the competitors as a whole; so that each competitor has to pick, not those faces which he himself finds prettiest, but those which he thinks likeliest to catch the fancy of the other competitors, all of whom are looking at the problem from the same point of view. It is not a case of choosing those which, to the best of one's judgment, are really the prettiest, nor even those which average opinion thinks the prettiest. We have reached the third degree where we devote our intelligences to anticipating what average opinion expects the average opinion to be. And there are some, I believe, who practice the fourth, fifth, and higher degrees [Keynes, *The General Theory of*

Employment Interest and Money, Harcourt Brace Jovanovich 1936].

Let's apply Keynes's metaphor to the current markets. Today we have more people playing the markets and greater diversity of personalities than ever before. (Traditionally, it was mostly lions playing the market and running the big firms. Now, there are nearly 100 million participants in the market. There are only about 50 million lions in the United States, so that means half the market now is nonlion.) Imagine Keynes's beauty contest with all white females and white males as beauties and judges, respectively. This was like the market of the mid-20th century in America: mostly lion investors buying lion-run companies. Now, enter some diversity. Imagine that the females pictured are equally divided between Caucasian, African, Asian, and Indian. Likewise, the judges are equally divided. If a Caucasian male did not alter his approach to the market based on the new diversity, then he might well pick mostly Caucasian females, because he is used to that. He will lose because the winning pictures will probably reflect the new diversity of the group.

How does this metaphor relate to the current stock market? As noted earlier, investors with different styles are entering the markets and voting with their dollars. As in the beauty contest, this increasing diversity will cause different stocks to be winners.

Hence, it's important to understand the personalities of the new market players. We've discussed the lions earlier, but what of the other 50 million new players? What are their characteristics and how will their votes (i.e., dollars) affect the market?

Some useful generalizations can be drawn from the earlier discussion about personality styles. Whereas the MBTI identifies 16 unique personality styles, based on combinations of the eight types, a man named Keirsey developed a simpler scheme for dividing people into just four temperaments. (See David Keirsey's *Portraits of Temperament* (Prometheus Nemesis 1987).) Your temperament is determined from your Myers-Briggs type; it is not a separate evaluation. Here is the formula :

> If your four letters contain "N" and "T," then you are a rationalist ("owl").
> If your four letters contain "N" and "F," then you are an idealist ("dolphin").
> If your four letters contain "S" and "P," then you are an adventurer ("fox").
> If your four letters contain "S" and "J," then you are a guardian ("lion").

Each Myers-Briggs type will fall into one of these four temperaments. The temperaments go back 2,500 years to the time of the Greeks, where they were originally named after the gods and their characteristics. Keirsey took the original material and updated it to fit the MBTI. Using Keirsey's temperaments, we can describe four distinct kinds of investors, with different motivations and different approaches.

We start with a review of the lions, then discuss the other three types.

THE GUARDIAN (SJ): LIONS RULE THE KINGDOM

View of the market: *"It's a battle to be won by patience, precision, and discipline."*

This is the most common temperament in the financial world. Lions are left-brained. They are precise, practical, motivated, and efficient. In short, they get the job done. They make excellent generals and leaders. Their virtues include discipline and stabilizing influence. They respect tradition and rules. Their strong suit in investing is discipline and execution. Their investment style is often technical analysis, rule-oriented and disciplined.

Famous lion investors: Marty Zweig, David Dreman.

Likely roles in an investment firm: technician or fundamental analyst using traditional methods; institutional traders, leaders, and administrators.

These investors will gravitate toward anything that says, "I'm steady." They love order and consistency. Their first instinct with money is to conserve it. They are great savers. They are persuaded by data and logic. These investors tend to be the least risk tolerant. They like safety.

Do they have weaknesses? In their own eyes, not many and not much. Because our culture reinforces their values—precision, clarity, bottom-line attention—they tend to see their own behavior as ideal. Hence, their weaknesses are often inflexibility, lack of vision, or being stuck in the past. As the pace of change in the world increases daily, lions must be careful to keep a few visionaries on hand, intuitive people who naturally enjoy predicting the future.

What kind of stocks will lions buy? How will they affect the market?

Lions will continue to play by the traditional rules, the ones that have worked in the past. They will focus on P/E ratios, dividend discount models, technical rules, earnings growth, and so forth. They will resist the dot.com stocks and their valuations, which appear crazy to tradition-based lions. A recent *Wall Street Journal* article ("A Fund Manager Stick to His Values, Loses Customers," Jan. 3, 2000) quoted a value-oriented investor, probably a lion, and his reaction to the technology stocks:

> Yet the portfolio manager continues to shun nearly all technology stocks because they violate his "value" approach to investing, buying shares that he deems undervalued on the basis of such measures as price-to-earnings ratios. "The thought of buying such overpriced shares is something I'll never do," the bargain-hunter declares.

In the meantime, investors have pulled nearly half of their money out of this investor's fund.

Lions may become an endangered species in the financial world if the markets continue to morph and lions hold fast to their old ways. However, lions will look like heroes if the astronomic valuations fall apart and the "old" rules are restored. And, of course, those different opinions are what make a market.

THE RATIONALIST (NT): THE WISE OLD OWL

View of the market: *"It's a challenging puzzle to be solved."*

Rationalists are like wise old owls, hovering in the air, seeing the big picture. They integrate both left and right brain, critical thinking and creative ideas. Therefore, they are excellent strategists and model builders. Their investment strength is creative analysis and their style is often a mix of value and contrarian investing. They like to work with models—dividend discount and factor models in particular—and to hunt for out-of-favor, undervalued merchandise. Ralph Wanger is an owl. He likes to work with investment themes; that is, to start with the big picture and work down to individual stocks. Warren Buffett and Charlie Munger may well be owls, too. They are fiercely competitive, pragmatic, and contrarian. The owl's likely role in an investment firm is as a strategist, economist, or analyst.

What are the owl's possible weaknesses? Some owls may hover too far above the investment scene and therefore lose touch with reality. We all know investors who were way ahead of their time. In the 1980s, a popular theme was rebuilding the infrastructure of America. Analysts recommended cement companies as obvious choices, because roads and bridges were being rebuilt in huge numbers. As sound as the reasoning was, the money never seemed to show up in the earnings of the cement companies and their stocks drifted, yielding unexciting returns.

Unlike the traditional lions, though, owls can usually shift and stretch with the times. They appreciate new paradigms and the need for new strategies. An example of a "new paradigm" owl is Bill Miller at Legg Mason. He has an incredible winning streak of nine years straight beating the S&P 500—beating it by an average of 11 percent each year over the past four years. Though labeled a value investor, a *Wall Street Journal* article said that Miller:

> taps esoteric sources of inspiration far beyond the confines of Wall Street, largely through his association with the Santa Fe Institute, a nonprofit think tank that studies "complex adaptive systems." Mr. Miller, who is on the institute's board of trustees, says buttons and thread, and alluvial geography, as well as ants, are among the things he has found can be instructive in the realm of investing ["A Value-Fund's Chief Redefines the Term—with Soaring Results," *Wall Street Journal*, Dec. 31, 1999].

Owls like Bill Miller are more willing to take on risk. This attitude, combined with their pragmatic and competitive inclinations, make them formidable opponents in the market. They are not new players in the market, but they may become more visible as successful players in a market that is becoming impervious to traditional methods.

Lions and foxes are two temperaments that have always gravitated toward the market. What about the new players, called foxes and dolphins?

THE ADVENTURIST (SP): THE WILY FOX

View of the market: *"It's a fun game to be played with flair."*

Adventurists are wily foxes who love to use their resourceful, clever minds. They thrive on activity and competition. Like the rationalist, they integrate both the left and right brain hemispheres, seeking precision and detail (left brain) but preferring a go-with-the-flow approach to life (right brain). Of all the temperaments, they are the most comfortable with risk. They are great salespeople and storytellers. Their investment strengths are finding facts, digging for the data, taking action and risks. Their investment style leans toward momentum or growth stocks: day trading, arbitrage, venture capital, hedge funds . . . anything with a kick. They love action. They love to be in the game. They love riding the wave. They like to make an impact. High turnover is common in their portfolios.

Though we've already noted that Peter Lynch has all the eight traits of great investors, his basic temperament may be that of the fox. Lynch is famous for his dictum: "Know the company's story." In fact, he says all investors should be able to pass the "two-minute drill" on every stock they own. What is the two-minute drill? You should be able to give the guts of the stock's story in two minutes. Foxes love to tell stories.

Furthermore, Lynch is famous for getting to the mall to kick the tires and see the merchandise. Foxes like action. They are good at collecting data. Another piece of evidence that suggests Lynch is a fox is the condition of his office, piled high with paper and reports. Foxes prefer to go with the flow and are overly concerned with organization.

Foxes make good deal makers, brokers, and hedge-fund managers. They love making things happen. They love the attention that they receive when they are successful. Inside every fox is an ego crying out, "Look, I'm special!"

This last characteristic indicates a possible weakness of foxes: They can be reckless and impatient in their quest to make an impact and be noticed. Their comfort with risk can make them dangerously impulsive. The odds are that many of the rogue traders, like Nick Leeson at Baring Bank, were foxes. He was caught up in the thrill of the game, of winning, of adulation. Foxes earn and spend money to be admired.

As more foxes trade in the markets, valuations may get more

outrageous. The technology sector, which currently offers the chance for quick fortunes, is exactly the kind of action that foxes like, even after the lions have left the room with nosebleeds from the dizzying heights. Foxes like momentum and risk and attention. What better way to get it today than large positions in the dot.com companies?

Finally, let's look at the rarest animal in the investment scene, the idealistic dolphin.

THE IDEALIST (NF): THE COMPASSIONATE DOLPHIN

View of the market: *"It's a garden to be weeded and cultivated for growth."*

Dolphins are the rarest animals in the financial world. Right-brained and not especially concerned about money or competition, the market has not interested them much until lately. But now these do-gooders have found a strong passion in the market: socially conscious investing. They are buying stocks of companies that make the world a better place. These are creative and warm-hearted individuals who thrive on harmonious relationships. Their investment strength is a natural affinity for collaboration and intuition. They tend to build solid, trusting relationships and to rely on them for information and guidance. If two heads are better than one, then dolphins have this advantage.

Their investment style: socially conscious and intuitive (they may base picks on clues from astrology, psychics, tarot cards, the I Ching, etc.).

A prominent dolphin investment fund is Domini Social Investments. They call themselves "The Responsible Index Fund." They consider both social and environmental factors, as well as traditional return measures. The fund's performance has been excellent. Since its inception in 1991, the fund has outpaced the S&P 500

Jungian Archetype	Guardian	Rationalist	Adventurer	Idealist
Animal	*Lion (SJ)*	*Owl (NT)*	*Fox (SP)*	*Dolphin (NP)*
Market view	"It's a battle to be won by patience, precision, and discipline."	"It's a challenging puzzle to be solved."	"It's a fun game to be played with flair."	"It's a garden to be weeded and cultivated for growth."
Investment strength	Discipline and execution.	Creative analysis.	Fact-finding, risk seeking.	Collaboration and intuition.
Investment style	Technical, rules-oriented.	Value, quantification, contrarian.	Growth and arbitrage.	Socially conscious.
Investment roles	Traders, administrators.	Analysts, strategists, economists.	Researchers, brokers, hedge-fund managers.	Research directors, client relationship handlers.
Examples	Zweig, Dreman.	Buffett, Munger.	Lynch.	Diversity fund, Domini fund.

Disadvantages and weaknesses	Too rigid, clings to past.	Too theoretical, lacks data.	Too reckless, lacks patience.	Too idealistic, lacks toughness and objectivity.
Communication style	Comparative.	Conditional.	Anecdotal.	Metaphoric.
Time orientation	Past.	Infinite.	Present.	Future.
Needs	Membership.	Competency.	Freedom.	Meaning.
Risk profile	Risk-averse.	Risk-neutral.	Risk-seeking.	Risk-neutral.
Fears	Losing control.	Being judged incompetent.	Being constrained.	Being abandoned.
Financial propensity	To save, hoard.	To take, wrest.	To spend, dissipate.	To give, divest.

Figure 12.1 Financial profiles of the four temperaments.

slightly, which means that it has beaten 90 percent of all domestic equity funds. In so doing, it received Morningstar's highest rating of five stars.

Another dolphin strategy is investing in diversity. Dolphins like the people side of business and like to invest in companies that are compassionate and progressive in their treatment of employees. Hence, diversity-friendly companies are favorites of dolphins—and they too have been outperforming the market. *Fortune* magazine reports that "companies that pursue diversity outperform the S&P 500" (July 19, 1999).

Given the success of these dolphin strategies, what are the possible pitfalls for dolphin investors? They are the most idealistic, and therefore most gullible, of all the temperaments. They tend to trust people too quickly, which leaves them vulnerable to ripoffs. Also, they tend to lack the objectivity that would allow them to see past emotional issues in some investments. An example? Some dolphins might object to investing in a company that is downsizing, arguing that its poor treatment of employees disqualifies it from consideration.

Figure 12.1 summarizes the financial profile of each of the four temperaments. Readers who find this particularly interesting can explore it in more depth in a book called *The Social Meaning of Money and Property* by Kenneth Doyle (Sage Publications 1999).

Chapter 13 examines how this material can be useful with your financial clients.

Temperament and Client Service

I don't know what your destiny will be, but one thing I know: the only ones among you who will be really happy are those who will have sought and found how to serve.

—Albert Schweitzer

Although the primary purpose of this book is to help investors in their thinking and decision making, the framework of personality styles is especially powerful in client relationships. If you've worked your way to this point, you have a pretty good understanding of personality types. Therefore, it would be a shame not to show how these tools can be used to serve clients in the financial field. Readers who don't act in this capacity may want to skip this chapter, but first consider that these tools are equally important in discussions with spouses, significant others, relatives, friends, and children. Money is one of touchiest subjects in our personal lives and the following material is designed to make the conversation smoother.

For starters, have your clients (or family members) take the MBTI. I realize that you may get resistance to this. You may hear something like, "I'm not crazy, I don't need a personality test." In almost every workshop I deliver, one person refuses to take the test because he or she sees it as an invasion of privacy. Fair enough; I don't argue with them. But when it comes to your clients, if you can gain their confidence and get them to take it, then you will have a blueprint for successful communication with them.

Here are some tips on doing that. First off, it's free and only takes five minutes. (Earlier in the book I gave the Website address.) Remind your clients that this test will help ease their financial fears. A good way to introduce the idea is to tell clients that you want to work effectively and smoothly with them and that this will really aid the process. If you emphasize the common goal of a successful, constructive meeting, it may help overcome some initial client resistance.

Money matters are extremely sensitive areas of our lives. When cash is the topic, many of us brace our bodies as if the dentist had just turned on the high-speed drill. We can't help it; we carry all kinds of baggage from our past. ("Money is the root of all evil," "It's easier for a camel to pass through the eye of a needle than for a rich man to get into heaven," "Money doesn't grow on trees," etc.) Be prepared to tread lightly through this "mindfield."

Imagine, though, the advantage of having a map for getting through this treacherous terrain. Importantly, the MBTI gives you a customized map, because each temperament relates differently to money.

Here are some tips for dealing with clients (or loved ones) based on personality style.

- If you are discussing money with introverts (I), give them time to digest what you are saying. Remember, their preference is to process internally, not out loud. They may need some silence to think through the implications. Also, introverts like to read, so perhaps you could write out your points and send them in advance. If you are requesting information from an introvert, you may want to have her write it on a form rather than speaking it. Introverts feel more comfortable organizing their thoughts on paper.

- The opposite applies to extraverts (E). Talk things through with them. Don't involve them in a lot of reading and writing; it's better to do it face-to-face. Reassure them that everything is on the table, that there are no hidden agendas.

- If you are meeting with a sensing (S) type to discuss finances, provide all the details in a logical, step-by-step fashion. Stick with concrete, real examples. Avoid hypotheticals that involve imaginary scenarios. Often a sensing type will assume that you are giving a real example and will become confused. (If you say, "Joe will have to pay capital gains tax if he sells his winning stocks," a sensor may respond, "Wait a minute, who is Joe?" To which you respond, "No one, I'm just making up a situation." At which point the sensor may furrow his brow and ask, "Why are you making up stories about my money?") It's also best to avoid metaphors, such as "Imagine that your dividend check is like a river flowing into a lake." They may not understand why you are talking about the environment when they have important money matters to tackle.

- Intuitives (N) need the opposite treatment. Give them the big picture and don't worry about details. If you can draw them a picture or paint a verbal picture of their scenario, and it hits home for them, you've struck gold. They will love it and refer back to it. Example: "Some stocks are like baseball singles, others are like home runs. Some of your money will be safe swings, some will be swinging for the fences." Intuitives like to talk about possibilities and the future and are comfortable jumping from one topic to another, so strict agendas are not important.

Thinking (T) and feeling (F) is probably the most important distinction in financial management. This difference will affect the whole tone of the conversation. Thinkers, with their detached and objective view, can come off as blunt and insensitive. Feelers, in contrast, can come across to thinkers as tenderhearted or fuzzy thinkers, not to be taken seriously. The problem lies in their core beliefs about cooperation and competition. Feelers tend to be cooperative, thinkers competitive.

So who is right, the thinker or the feeler? No doubt, based on the inclusive premise of this book, you know that both are, depending on the circumstances. It's not either/or but rather both/and. They are both necessary and useful inclinations, but in very different settings. I call them "tough" and "tender" ethics. Another way to look at them is golden gloves or golden rule. The golden glove ethics are "tough," the golden rule "tender." Tender ethics are necessary and useful in client (or personal) relationships where the client's interest comes first. Tough ethics are necessary in the capital markets where "perform or die" is the rule, as Ralph Wanger says.

The truly excellent professional investor would develop skills in both tough and tender ethics. To help clarify this tender/tough distinction, Figure 13.1 lists a set of characteristics for each.

Tough (Thinking preference)	Tender (Feeling preference)
Competitive.	Cooperative.
Performance-oriented.	Relationship-oriented.
Seek win-lose outcomes.	Seek win-win outcomes.
Value competence.	Value compassion.
Song: *We Are the Champions.*	Song: *All You Need is Love.*
Motto: Let the buyer beware.	Motto: The customer is always right.
Heroes: General Patton, Warren Buffett.	Heroes: Gandhi, Martin Luther King, Jr.
College major: business.	College major: liberal arts.

Figure 13.1   Characteristics of tough versus tender preferences.

The last distinction in this grid of contrasts—college major— provides a good example of how the two types clash. Each semester Ken Doyle, professor of journalism and mass communication at the University of Minnesota, fills his classroom with half business students and half liberal arts majors and shows the movie *Wall Street*. Gordon Gekko, the tycoon who proclaims that "greed is good," fascinates the business students. They take notes on his tactics. They relish his "take no prisoners" attitude. This same Gekko repulses the liberal arts students, who delight in watching his demise. Afterward, the liberal arts students invariably express the desire to shower and scrub with soap. The point of the exercise is not to debate which set of attitudes is "right," but rather to see them clearly and explore the differences. In fact, this distinction between tough and tender is as basic as parenting: the balance of tough love and tender love for a child. Parents continually wrestle with the right amount of discipline versus nurturing.

Professional investors, then, must blend the best of thinkers and feelers and use each skill appropriately. Figure 13.2 shows how this is done. When investors are dealing in the markets, they are expected to be knowledgeable ("expert") and tough ("thinking"). When dealing with clients, who occupy one of the other three boxes, investors must use the golden rule and put the client's interest first. This balance is tricky, as proven by the high annual incidence of

	Novice (Low)	Expert (High)
Thinking (tough-minded)	Novice and tough (exploit ignorance).	Expert and tough (fair fight).
Feeling (tender-minded)	Novice and tender (exploit both).	Expert and tender (exploit trust).

Figure 13.2   Knowledge of investing/temperament types.

investment practitioners who get their wrists slapped for exploit-
ing the trust of their clients.

The final set of preferences, disciplined (judging, J) versus flexible (perceiving, P), will determine the flow of the client conversation. Judgers like closure. They like to see bullet points, plans, and
action steps. They don't want limitless alternatives. They don't like
living with uncertainty. They will appreciate a clear recommendation or a few clearly defined options.

Perceivers, in contrast, are much more comfortable with the
give-and-take of new information, different options, and unresolved
items. They don't need schedules and agendas for goals. If things
are heading in the right direction, that's good enough. Their
attitude is: Let's not tie ourselves down. Freedom is keeping the
door open.

The preceding tips should help in dealing with financial matters, both professionally and personally, but even more important
are the following comments about temperaments. As discussed
earlier, a person's temperament reflects his or her core needs, values, and—all-importantly—fears. Given our fragile human condition, nothing motivates us like fear. Advertisers play on it all the
time, sometimes very subtly, sometimes not. The more you know
someone's hot buttons, the better the odds are that you can influence that person. Cynics would say, "The better you know someone, the more you can manipulate them." But this truth can, just
as validly, be reframed as: "The more I know about a person, the
more I can help him or her." How? By designing their investments
according to that individual's preferences and needs and by com-
municating in a way that suits the person's temperament. Here are
some guidelines by temperament:

- If your client (or family member) is a lion (SJ), then his or
  her core needs revolve around tradition and membership.
  Lions value rules, regulations, security, and stability. They

tend to be very good protectors and providers for their families. The recommended approach is to help them feel secure about their finances. They want to know that they can protect and provide for their family's financial needs. They project an image of "I'm steady" to the world. Their big fear is losing control. The more you can do to present an image of solid, stable, time-tested financial management, the more they will appreciate it. Titles are important, so display any degrees or titles prominently. The major cautions are these. Don't get too theoretical. Remember that these are sensing types; they like things practical and grounded. Don't try new, untested, or risky investment strategies; remember that these people tested and proven techniques. Don't appear carefree and cavalier; these types appreciate a strong, serious work ethic.

- Clients who are owls (NTs) have core needs that include mastery and knowledge. They value expertise, intelligence, ingenious concepts, and progress. They tend to be competitive and will test your knowledge (unlike the lions, who will assume that you are the expert unless you show them otherwise). To owls, this is a game to see if you are competent and smart. You must respond to this challenge by showing that you are indeed up to the task of defending your ideas and positions. The correct response to a challenge is to respond in kind. The owl will respect you for your competence and knowledge. Owls try to project an image of "I'm a winner." Money is a means to show this, usually through status-symbol property items. Owls are not afraid of risk, so their portfolios can be tilted toward some high-return assets, like venture capital and technology stocks. Their attitude toward money is to take it from others, as a symbol of winning. Their greatest fear is to be judged incompetent. They hate losing and feeling needy. When you work with owls, show them your own competence and let them know that you, too, are a winner. This is not the group to show your weak side to. They won't be inclined to "rescue" you. They will instead find a new—competent—account manager.

- The foxes (SPs) are yet another profile, altogether different from lions and owls. The core need of a fox is freedom. They love to act on impulse and to make an impact. They value action and adventure. Hence, the approach with foxes is much different. They will want to be entertained. They want variety; they want an adrenaline rush. If you use the lion strategy (stable, solid, secure), you will bump up against the fox's big fear: being bored. A fox projects the image, "Look, I'm special!" They don't want to simply live an ordinary, decent life. They like charisma and good stories. They spend money to be admired, and they take risks. As their financial adviser, you will want to build an element of adventure into their portfolios. You want to give them a bit of Las Vegas, without jeopardizing their future. Perhaps you would invest a small portion of their funds in very high-risk vehicles, like hedge funds and options, or other investments that move every day.

- The final temperament, the dolphin (NF), is the least interested in money. Their core need is about finding the meaning of life and establishing a unique identity. They value authenticity, ethics, relationships, and cooperation. Their primary use for money is to do good in the world. Their relationship to money usually involves giving it away, partially to reinforce their self-image, which is "I'm wholesome." They also use money to create safety: warm, nurturing family and friendly relationships. They do not pride themselves on having lots of money. Hence, the owl tactic of using money as a badge of success doesn't work at all for dolphins. The main fear for dolphins is isolation or abandonment. The best way to get them interested in their financial lives—often they don't care—is to link financial well-being with family happiness and charity. If the success of their portfolio will allow them to help their family and those in need, then they will see financial growth as a positive. Otherwise, they tend to view wealth as unimportant or even downright evil.

The more you can reassure dolphins that you will be there to help them and take care of their money concerns, the more they will trust and like you. Taking an interest in them as people, their families and their hobbies, is an excellent way to build rapport with dolphins. Relationships with dolphins may have little to do with their portfolio and everything to do with trust and friendship. Whatever you do, don't schmooze dolphins. They will run, not walk, away from anything wearing a plaid jacket and cowboy boots. They appreciate simplicity, authenticity, and honesty.

Briefly, those are the guidelines for dealing with money and relationships. As you can see, the way different types relate to money is completely different; using the simple guidelines listed in this chapter will open huge opportunities for you. As you begin to recognize and understand different types, you will gain skill in handling them differently and effectively. Just as you would care for a goldfish very differently from a German shepherd, likewise you would treat an owl investor very differently from a fox.

Having briefly visited the use of temperament with client relationships, we now expand our discussion of investment collaboration to investigate how investment teams can become more creative.

The Creative Investment Team: Tools for Enhancing Creativity

CHAPTER 14

Brainstorming for the Masses

People's problems are forcing them to work together, and they are recognizing that. The problems they have result from a whole set of interdependencies that force them to work together.
—Peter Senge, MIT

The first process for unleashing an organization's creativity is so simple and so powerful that you would think every major organization would use it monthly. Some do, but most don't. Go figure. The door is wide open for you and your investment group to take full advantage of this process, thereby crushing the competition like insects under your bootheels and . . . well, you get the idea.

The process is called Open Space and it was introduced by Harrison Owen, a clergyman turned consultant. Based on the theories of self-organizing systems, proposed by Meg Wheatley, Peter Senge, and others, Open Space is the right-brained (NFP) response to a left-brained (STJ) world. The American population is dominated by sensing (S), thinking (T), and judging (J) personalities, not only in terms of sheer numbers—there *are* more of them—but culturally as well. Most organizations, including schools, businesses, investment shops (as discussed earlier), hospitals, and so on, are run by STJ rules. What does that mean? William Bridges, author of *The Character of Organizations* (Davies-Black 1992), writes of STJ organizations that:

Logic and good sense appeal to them. Intuition and radical innovations make them nervous. Internally, STJ organizations are likely to be organized functionally and to provide people with clear expectations and role responsibilities. In big organizations, this tendency can produce a collection of somewhat isolated domains between which communication is difficult.

STJ organizations like schedules and control and thrive on order. Imagine, then, what an NFP process would look like: a coffee break. *Huh?* Yes, an extended coffee break. People would mingle, munch on snacks, talk freely, and shift from one conversation to another as the spirit moved them. Well, that was the inspiration for Owen's Open Space process. He noticed that the most valuable part of big conferences was the coffee break between sessions:

> In 1983, I had occasion to organize an international conference for 250 participants. It took me a full year of labor. By the time I had finished with all the details, frustrations, and egos (mine and others') that go with such an event, I resolved never to do such a thing again. This resolution was confirmed at the conclusion of the conference, when it was agreed by one and all (including myself) that although the total event had been outstanding, the truly useful part had been the coffee breaks [Owen, *Open Space Technology: A User's Guide*, Berrett-Koehler 1997].

So, Owen asked himself, how can we construct an eight-hour coffee break? And the answer was Open Space. The process is so simple and natural that those of us who have complicated our lives almost beyond redemption can't, at first, grasp it. In Open Space, you simply let people follow their passions. You let them talk about issues that really matter to them. You also follow Owen's guideline that "if it isn't fun, it isn't working."

What is the process?

It begins with an invitation to all concerned parties (stakeholders) to attend the meeting. It is strictly voluntary. This is the first important departure from STJ meetings, which are usually mandatory. The invitation includes the theme for the meeting and the time and place. Second key difference at the Open Space meeting? No agenda. (You can almost hear the shriek from the STJ population: "What! No schedule? Surely chaos will follow!") Right. Constructive chaos.

Instead of a set agenda as people enter the meeting room, the participants are asked to develop their own, based on the real interests and needs of the people in attendance. Whenever I've explained this process to STJ "lion" managers, they invariably blanch and raise a hundred objections. A popular objection is that the meeting will career into chaos, with the whiners taking over and running an all-day bitch session. Despite this universal STJ concern, it has never happened in my experience or to any of my colleagues who've run these sessions.

A third aspect of Open Space that runs counter to lion management norms is the circular seating arrangement. As people enter the room, someone always murmurs, "Looks like we're going to be asked to take off our shoes, do some sharing, and then sing 'Kumbaya.'" Not likely. The circle is an ancient symbol of many things, one of them being equality. In Open Space, lion leaders are asked to put aside their authority roles and just participate as ordinary employees. The role of the outside facilitator is specifically to make sure that this happens. (Lion leaders who can't seem to get the hang of letting go of power are referred to as "space invaders." Part of the training for facilitators is learning how to gracefully remove the kings from their highchairs.)

Open Space is driven by two forces: personal responsibility and passion. Because attendance is voluntary, none of the participants can escape the call for each person to take responsibility for his or her experience. Presumably they came to the meeting because they had some conviction about the topic: raising profitability, building a better mousetrap, enhancing team morale, finding a new investment idea, whatever. If not, they shouldn't have come.

The day (or days—an Open Space session can go up to three

days) consists of creating an agenda of topics, all of which relate to the general theme, and scheduling times for the topics to be discussed. The people who originally suggested the topic are asked to be the conveners of that session, which means that they take notes and provide a summary report of what ideas were discussed and any action steps decided on.

Does it work? (A good left-brained question!)

I asked this question of Harrison Owen when I met him in the spring of 1998. He was conducting a training for Open Space facilitators at St. Mary's Retreat Center in Mundelein, Illinois. I found him walking in the woods, smoking a cigarette, staring at a buck a few hundred yards away. When I spoke to Harrison, the buck looked up and gracefully bounded out of view.

"So, are there any success stories from Open Space events?" I asked, wearing my skeptic's hat.

"Depends how you define success," he said. This is a typical response from an NFP personality. Sometimes I think "NFP" stands for "No Firm Positions." Other times, I'm convinced it stands for "Not for Profit." Either way, Open Space has been used for many purposes, from corporate initiatives to the reorganization of a major religious denomination. But I was interested in the kind of success that lions could relate to.

"Corporate success. Getting the job done efficiently and saving money," I answered.

"Sure," he said, finishing his cigarette and tossing it aside. "Coca Cola at the 1996 Olympics in Atlanta. They spent several months constructing their exhibit booth, which would entertain about 5,000 people each day. Then the Olympic committee saw it and praised it so highly that they asked Coke to move it to center stage. The problem for Coke was that it had taken them over six months to design and build the booth. And at this point, there were only about eight weeks before the Olympics. So, the booth that was built over a period of months to host 5,000 people, now had to be redesigned and rebuilt for ten times that number of people in less time. The people at Coke called me in to help. The level of urgency was perfect for Open Space. I knew it would work. It always does when there is real work to be done, and lots of passion. These people were very motivated."

"And how did it turn out?" I said.

"Fine. They did a three-day Open Space and completely redesigned the exhibit booth. They finished setting it up with time to spare."

"So the work that had taken months was reduced to three days?"

"Yes."

Impressive. And simple. Harness people's passion and let them go to work. As General Patton said about military leadership, tell the troops which hill to take but not how to take it. Leaving motivated people to their own devices is a first-rate strategy for success.

There are many other Open Space success stories, some from the investment world. I was asked to facilitate an Open Space with the information technology (IT) department of a major money manager. The leaders nearly passed out when I first told them my plan (or lack thereof!). They didn't see how a day that started with no agenda could lead to anything constructive and focused. What made matters worse was that this planning meeting included consultants from another firm, who had a different product to sell. They continued to throw gasoline on the fire each time the investment leaders raised a concern.

"This open meeting idea sounds like it will turn into an all-day bitch session," said the leaders.

"Right," said the consultants, "there's too much negativity in the department. Without a vision and focused discussion, you'll just make things worse." (Three guesses what the other consultants were selling: vision and mission workshops.)

Well, I prevailed; the leaders reluctantly decided to go with Open Space as a format. The night before the session I got exactly zero hours of sleep. Despite all the successes that I'd experienced personally and heard about from others, I kept thinking, "This will be the one time it doesn't work." But true to form, Open Space did work. The participants rolled up their sleeves and got right to work addressing and resolving the issues that most concerned them. The degree of honesty was surprising and refreshing. Here are some comments from participants at the meeting:

> "[A]n effective way to take controversial issues and deal with them in a constructive and creative way."
>
> From the leader: "I didn't know what to expect, but this process really helped get people focused and motivated. We had lots of good discussions and made progress on key issues."

The literature on Open Space now contains 10 years' worth of data and many success stories from major companies such as US West and Boeing, as well as government, not-for-profits, and religious organizations.

What is the point of bringing up Open Space in a book about investing? Just this. Despite many inquiries to practitioners of Open Space, I have yet to find one that has worked with a major investment firm or investment club. Given that information and rigorous discussion are the lifeblood of successful investment decisions, it strikes me as unusual that this process has never been employed. Furthermore, the four conditions required for Open Space seem ideally suited to the investment field:

1. Complexity. The problem being addressed must be complex and multifaceted. Isn't this the very nature of the markets? The mix of so many variables and so many approaches to valuation and asset allocation is the core problem that investors face.
2. Adversity. There must be different interest groups to bump up against one another. Well, by definition, any investment

organization worth its salt will have disagreements and conflict amongst the different asset groups, functional groups, regions, and so on.

3. Diversity. The participants must be sufficiently different, either in thinking styles, ethnicity, approaches, backgrounds, or other attributes. Given the global nature of investing these days, the diversity continues to grow.

4. Urgency. The problem being addressed must be urgent. The participants want a solution and they want it quickly. This is the fuel that pushes a successful Open Space. Otherwise it is just an interesting exercise, a lively chat, a bull session. Have you ever been on a trading floor? Is investing a climate of urgency?

These are the four conditions for a successful Open Space. I submit that it is a perfect process for investment firms, and that many of them should pursue this simple but profound approach.

What gets in the way? One obstacle is the introverted nature of many investment professionals. They prefer to work alone, shunning meetings and formal gatherings. They also tend to distrust outsiders coming into their environs and foisting anything that smacks of touchy-feely onto them. (Is the opposite of touchy-feely *stuffy-thinky*? Just wondering.)

Perhaps, though, at a deeper level, the very nature of investing runs counter to a big open meeting. After all, investing is much like gambling. Poker players are taught the value of information (their cards) and to hold them close to the vest. The last thing you would do as an expert card player is show everyone your hand and exchange trade secrets (such as when you usually bluff, what you'll open betting with, what body language you display when you're about to fold, etc.)

This fact was brought home to me the first time I attended a noninvestment conference. The meeting was organized by a group called American Productivity and Quality Center (APQC) and featured speakers from many top organizations talking on the subject of innovation. The meeting sessions were normal enough, but my entire paradigm for conferences was blown sky-high during the cocktail hour. Attendees were—even now I shudder when I think of it—openly sharing the secrets of their businesses with one another. I wanted to jump on one of the hors d'oeuvres tables and shout, "Come to your senses, people, you're giving all the goodies away!" My silent thought was, "Are these people just stupid?" I could not understand it. From my background, where one slip in the trading room meant that someone would front-run your major buy program, I just didn't understand. It was one of those memorable moments where an old mental model audibly collapses.

For these reasons, I think the investment industry has yet to take advantage of the right-brained technology of Open Space. Nevertheless, the day is already here when they could benefit from it. All of the changes in the industry necessitate immediate decisions made with the highest quality of available thinking. It would not be unreasonable to envision a day when a major investment firm holds an Open Space-type meeting quarterly, in the same way that board meetings are held each quarter.

How does one conduct an Open Space meeting? Go to the Website, <www.openspaceworld.org>, and inquire about a facilitator. Or simply pick up the book, *Open Space Technology: A User's Guide*, by Harrison Owen and read it. The process is so simple that any competent facilitator could oversee it.

Having opened the discussion of how investment firms can become more creative, we now examine the optimal environment for innovation.

CHAPTER 15

The Creative Investor

Taming the Critics

I find the pain of little censure, even when it is unfounded, is more acute than the pleasure of much praise.

—Thomas Jefferson

Before jumping into the guidelines for creative collaboration, I want to make a simple point. Simple and all-important. *Creativity requires a safe environment.* Safe to be natural and unguarded. Safe to make mistakes. And safety, like charity, begins at home. So how does one create an inner sense of safety?

I'm amazed that so few books on creativity address this question. Even really good books—like the latest one by Michael Michalko, *Cracking Creativity* (Ten Speed Press 1998)—don't address it. Michalko mentions it in one line, in the section on brainstorming: "You turn off your internal critic." Great. How does one do that? Covering it in one line is a bit like a coach saying to a basketball player, "Hey, please score 40 points in the fourth quarter." It's reminiscent of Will Rogers's advice to an aspiring investor: "Buy the stocks that go up. If they don't go up, don't buy them!"

The inner critic is the single biggest barrier to creativity. Therefore, before we leap ahead to a discussion of group creativity, it's important to cover the individual aspects of the process. How do you create safety within yourself? How do you tame the internal critic that gets its jollies by calling you stupid, denigrating your work, and tearing apart your best ideas? This topic is tricky because often the inner critic, like a hidden addiction, is cunning, baffling, and powerful. It works behind the scenes, quietly undermining your confidence and keeping your creativity at bay.

Sadly, many people live their entire lives without realizing this. It's like owning a car for 10 years and never knowing that the parking brake was on the entire time. Your car would have been so much faster and more efficient if only you had been aware of the problem and dealt with it! Instead, the car handled poorly and burned up lots of extra gasoline.

How do we recognize and deal with the inner critic?

Of all the material available for enhancing creativity, one of the most powerful is a book by two psychologists, Hal Stone and Sidra Stone, called *Embracing Your Inner Critic* (HarperCollins 1992). The subtitle is interesting for our purposes: *Turning Self-Criticism into a Creative Asset*. Why is the inner critic so harmful? Here is the list that the Stones call the "Top Twelve Traits of the Inner Critic." As you can see, it starts with how damaging the critic is to creativity and risk-taking:

1. It constricts your ability to be creative.
2. It stops you from taking risks because it makes you fear failure.
3. It views your life as a series of mistakes waiting to happen.
4. It undermines your courage to change.
5. It compares you unfavorably with others and makes you feel inferior.
6. It is terrified of being shamed and monitors all your behavior to avoid this.
7. It causes you to suffer from low self-esteem, and possibly

depression, because it tells you that you are not good enough.

8. It can make looking at yourself in a mirror or shopping for clothes miserable because of its ability to create such a negative view of the body.

9. It can take all the fun out of life with its criticisms.

10. It makes self-improvement a compulsive chore because it bases the work on the premise that something is wrong with you.

11. It doesn't allow you to acknowledge or accept the good feelings that other people have toward you.

12. It makes you susceptible, and often victim, to the judgments of other people.

Reading this book was a major turning point for me. I had been trying for years to turn off my internal critic. I knew that it was dampening my creativity and lowering my energy level, but there seemed to be little or no good advice available. Suggestions ranged from "Don't pay any attention to the internal critic" to "Tell the internal critic to shut up!" One seemed like denial, the other like throwing gasoline on the fire. Wasn't there some middle way?

The Stones had a very different approach, which worked for me. The Stones acknowledge the inner critic that lives within all of us (Freud called it the *superego*) and provide a process for transforming it into an ally.

As I read the Stones' book, I realized that the inner critic was like a compulsive habit for me. I couldn't seem *not* to listen to it. I couldn't shut it off. Like the drug addict who knows that heroin is destroying him, but uses it anyway, I judged myself continually.

Why would I—or anyone—do that? It seems so stupid and unproductive. This is the part of the Stones' explanation that I found unusually insightful. They believe that our internal critic is actually a misguided ally, trying to help us; rather than some evil spirit trying to destroy us. The critic is reacting to early life experiences and messages from our parents and others. Like a software program that gets written before we have a say in it, the critic learns what will keep us safe. Unless you had one of the mythical "good enough" parents, your inner critic probably has been giving you a lot of bogus messages about playing it safe, looking good, staying in control, and the like. Mostly these messages were useful only in our families of origin, where we were "guests" of our parents and had to play by their rules. As we grow up and go out into the world, these rules don't serve us anymore. If we are going to shine creatively, we have to stop seeking approval and being terrified of rejection, and trust our own intuition.

Put simply, the critic is trying to protect us. Its job is to keep us safe, to keep us alive. It's in this sense that the critic is the enemy of creativity. Why? Think for a second of a child's world. Parents and school officials teach that conformity is good ("color within the lines"). Thus, children in our society associate being different with being bad or wrong. They receive disapproving looks from parents and questions like, "Why can't you be like the others?"

Why is being bad or wrong so scary? Well, those traits—thinks the child—could lead to rejection by parents, teachers, and classmates. Rejection for a child means being alone or uncared for. And—here's the key step in the logical progression—being uncared for as a child means death. Not figuratively, but literally. Small children are terrified of abandonment because it means they will die. So, this progression goes all the way from being different to death. I believe that this "different = death" equation is what propels much of the critic's "life-saving" behavior. The critic's job is to keep us the same.

How does this old software program in our psyche still run our lives today? The critic doesn't go away just because we grow up. Like a dog that is trained to bark at strangers, it continues that behavior forever until it is retrained not to do it. Recently, I talked with a successful, middle-aged money manager who would love to leave the big, bureaucratic firm that he works for and start his own practice. Why doesn't he? He's scared. His critic is still barking like mad every time this man contemplates "being different" and leaving the traditional path. (The critic views leaving as death and then subtly—remember the critic is smart—gives you all the cogent reasons why you should stay: five weeks' paid vacation, matching 401(k) benefit, great health plan, and on and on. This man's critic is so smart that he actually ends up boasting about how great he has it in his current job, even though at other times he's quite despondent.) What should the man do? Who knows? But I will tell you one thing for sure: he won't realize his creative potential where he is. And that's a shame, because he is naturally creative and brilliant (INTP). This man has admitted privately that he won't be proud of his safe career once he's old and retired and reviewing his life, after it's too late to change anything.

What can be done? To show you how the process of transforming the critic into an ally works, I'll use myself as an example. I had a nasty critic for most of my adult life. True, in many ways it helped me build a good résumé, with high marks, good schools, promotions, and the like, but I wasn't having much fun doing it, and I certainly wasn't tapping into my full creativity. In fact, one of my first bosses pulled me aside on my second day of employment and said, "We like people who don't rock the boat." This proved true. A few months later, I got dirty looks for bringing in the first computer to the office. The culture was control-and-command oriented. Very conservative, very risk-averse. But I stayed there because it was safe and lucrative. Sound familiar?

Understanding your critic is essential to freeing your creativity. Ask yourself, "In what ways do I criticize myself? What fears arise if I think of leading a much more adventurous, risky life? What beliefs do I hold that limit my creativity?"

The Stones divide critics into three categories: lightweights, middleweights, and heavyweights. They believe that "Heavyweight Critics just hate us. They want us dead."

The process for change that the Stones recommend—and it worked for me—is called Voice Dialogue. It can be verbal, with a friend or counselor, or written in the form of a journal. The essence of the process is simple: Treat your own internal critic like a person who needs a sympathetic ear. Listen with the same concern and attention that you would give to a friend or child who was describing a problem. The key is to remain neutral and not get pulled into the drama. This point is critical. (Sorry, no pun intended.)

The process can get a little tricky here. The Aware Ego is the conscious part of the psyche, the part that separates us from the animal kingdom and allows us to "watch" our moods, thoughts, and sensations. (This notion of the Aware Ego was playfully dealt with in a Seinfeld episode in which George referred to himself in the third person: "George doesn't like it when he doesn't get his way . . . ") One way to experiment with the Aware Ego is to write an account of your day in the third person. Imagine watching yourself go through the day and instead of writing, "then I went to the mall . . . ", write "then Sally went to the mall . . . " When I made this switch in my journaling it helped tremendously. I was able to stay neutral and take a sincere interest in the critic's comments and what concerns underlay them. Otherwise, I would continually take the bait and end up in a battle. The critic, being part of you, knows exactly what your weak points are. It can hook you faster than a fly fisherman. My critic would say things to me like, "You call *that* a workout? You only ran one mile. Who are you kidding? You shouldn't have bothered." To which I would respond smartly, "Cram it. One mile is plenty. I read in a health magazine that 20 minutes of daily exercise is plenty, so shut up." And we were off to the races.

Switching to the Aware Ego point of view, it was easier for me instead to respond, "What's your point here? Why are you attacking?"

Invariably the answer to this question involved the critic's fear that somehow "Jim's" behavior had put everybody in danger. Critics respond to fear. That's when they attack. That's also why it is so hard for people to change: because all change involves fear, and fear activates the critic. The critic, being clever and knowledgeable about all your weak spots, will convince you to stay put. Change is tough because you are battling a worthy opponent—*and creativity is a form of change*, a new way of seeing things. Therefore, creativity is nearly impossible if you have a strong inner critic.

The strategy for transforming the critic is to assume a neutral position and listen to the critic rant until the energy shifts and the soft underbelly is revealed. It takes patience and discipline. Here's an actual excerpt from my journal:

Aware Ego: So, how are you feeling about Jim today?

Critic: I'm disgusted with him, he's a spineless coward.

Aware Ego: How so?

Critic: On the phone today with that client, Jim completely folded. Anyone could have stood up to that bully. But not Jim. Instead, he tries to make the guy his best friend. The fool. He's such a phony. I'm ashamed of him.

Aware Ego: So, you think Jim is a phony?

Critic: Oh God, don't start that psychobabble crap with me. You sound like Jim when he facilitates off-sites. He can use that horse dung with his clients but don't sling it around here. I'll puke.

(This sort of venting continues for several pages and then the tone changes.)

Aware Ego: It sounds like you're scared.

Critic: I am scared. Jim left a perfectly good job and is trying to run his own business. But there's no way of knowing if it will work. And there is no steady check coming in. And that client who was upset today is the biggest source of revenue. Jim should have handled that better, he should have known his material better, he should have followed up sooner. I'm just really scared that this isn't going to work. I mean he's up against the big boys now. You can't fake it when there's just you. He's out there for everyone to see.

Aware Ego: Is there something that Jim could do to make you feel safer?

Critic: Yes, he could get some more clients. At least try. He's been hanging out with his friends and family and letting the marketing slide. He needs to keep his eye on the business.

Aware Ego: A marketing plan would make you feel safer?

Critic: Absolutely.

As I developed the ability to simply listen objectively to my internal critic, some remarkable changes took place. I felt less critical of myself and others. I began to see all critical attacks as calls for help. This reframing is particularly helpful in relationships. When I am tempted to criticize a friend or family member, I can step back and ask, "What am I feeling frightened about? How am I feeling vulnerable?" In this way, our own inner critic becomes the spokesperson for our vulnerability. Listening and attending to these inner cries for help creates a safe space for us and enhances our capacity to be creative.

If one takes the time and energy to transform the inner critic, it can become the inner ally, with the following traits, again paraphrasing the Stones:

1. It acts like a positive coach who supports you, makes your risk taking safe, and allows you to be creative and flowing.
2. It is impersonal and does not allow you to worry about what others will think.
3. It helps you to set appropriate boundaries.
4. It is no longer interested in other people's criticisms, so they do not bother you. This helps to free you from the fear of shame or humiliation.
5. Its power gives you greater authority in the world.
6. It brings you the ability to focus clearly.
7. As an objective mind, it analyzes events and feelings coolly, without making either you or others wrong.

8. Its objective evaluations of situations help you to behave appropriately and with self-discipline.
9. It helps you to get appropriate consultation and advice without making you feel that this is a sign of inadequacy.
10. It can direct you to self-improvement as growth or as an adventure rather than as a chore, because nothing is "wrong" with you. It does not talk about symptoms or problems.

As I said earlier, in my own creative work this transformation from critic to ally has made all the difference. It has been hugely freeing. An example? I rarely suffer from the dreaded writer's block now. I can sit in front of a blank page, write for a while, set it aside, then read it, and calmly state, "Yuck, this is awful." In the past, I would have found diversions to keep me from even attempting the writing. Assuming that somehow I did manage to sit and create, I dreaded the inevitable two-hour critique that would follow. ("You call THAT an insightful piece of writing?! Blah, blah, blah . . . ") The result? Much lower creative output. Now, though, the process is very different, with the critic as ally. I enjoy the creative process. I know that sometimes I'll strike oil and sometimes it's a dry hole. Just keep drilling. Importantly, I don't get discouraged; I'm ready to try again later that day. Creating this personal safety has been the key.

A word of caution. I showed this material to a colleague in the money management business and his response was, "I don't have a problem censoring myself, I just let whatever I'm thinking fly." Right. He does. Because of this, his coworkers blanch at the thought of brainstorming with him. His internal critic becomes an external critic, slicing and dicing others at will. If a person has a critic—internal or external—that is running rampant, he won't foster a safe environment for creativity. He probably won't get the feedback that he needs to change anything, either. Why? Because he has already intimidated his coworkers, who are his main source of constructive feedback.

A perfect example of this occurred in a consultation with the head of a bond department. We were discussing this issue of safety and openness. She expressed concern that so few of her staff brought up fresh ideas in their meetings. She had already acknowledged that she could be hot-tempered at times. "Are the people on your staff naturally creative?" I asked. (I already knew the answer, because they had all taken the MBTI and three-quarters had shown a preference for intuition, which means seeing the big picture.)

"Yes," she responded.

"Well, why do you think they're holding back?" I asked.

Glancing at the clock and then her appointment book, this very bright woman said, "I don't know, but I'm getting tired of it." Then, rising out of her chair, placing both fists on her desk, she added, "And some of their precious little worlds are going to get rocked if nothing changes."

Yikes, I thought. I felt intimidated, and I wasn't even on her staff. Is there any question as to why the staff is reluctant to take risks?

Safety begins at home. Look at the behavior of your own critic before pointing fingers at others in our group.

Assuming that a measure of personal safety is present, how do we move from personal safety to group safety? That is the subject of Chapter 16.

Creating a Safe Place

Criticism should not be querulous and wasting, all knife and rootpuller, but guiding, instructive, inspiring.

—Ralph Waldo Emerson

How do we create safety in a group? How do we make it safe for open and honest conversation? I remember reading an article in the Chicago Business School magazine about brainstorming, in which a consultant from Andersen described an incredible "war room" that clients use for brainstorming. It had special whiteboards for capturing and printing ideas, teams of IT people behind the scenes calling up data as it was needed, ergonomically correct chairs . . . you name it, they had it. For these fancy digs, clients paid as much as $100,000 for a few days of brainstorming. I got discouraged reading it because my approach seemed so simple and folksy. No gadgets, no high-tech. (And a lot cheaper, I might add!) Then I read the last paragraph of the article, in which the consultant said, "All this fancy equipment is really for one purpose: to get people talking." Bingo. That is the heart of creativity: good, honest, open dialogue. And that occurs *only* if people feel safe. No profound breakthroughs will occur if people are in danger.

Does this mean that there must be no conflict? Does this mean that no one will feel scared?

No. Conflict is part of creativity. So is fear, at times. People will feel frightened as they go deeply into their creative spirits and touch new edges, especially when it involves revealing their weaknesses. Most of us—with the help of our crafty critics—spend our lives developing successful strategies for protecting the tender spots. We know how to appear smart, commanding, steady, "together." We know how to fit in and look good. But true creativity requires that you leave that need for approval behind, and the only way to do that in a group is by building trust and mutual respect. Most people have a best friend to whom they can tell anything and still be accepted; a creative group requires a similar level of unconditional acceptance.

In my experience, investment groups tend to be poor at creating safe spaces for creativity. Their lion-like, left-brained temperaments are focused on performance and competence. They want the right answer and they want it quickly. They want results. Above all, they don't want to look foolish. Foolish people get mocked, ignored, left behind, rejected. In fact, in a meeting with lions, if one of them does lower the shield just a bit, the others tend to converge on the vulnerable spot like sharks in a feeding frenzy. I saw this phenomenon repeatedly when I led diversity training for investment managers. Some poor soul, usually a secretary or support staff person, would bring up a personal life trauma—a divorce, a son's drug addiction, a bankruptcy—and the room temperature would drop ten degrees. Body language and mocking comments gave a clear signal: Don't go there. Don't make the rest of us feel uncomfortable.

A wonderfully ironic example of this occurred in my first diversity training. I had asked the group to do an exercise on stereotypes. They were to choose some commonly stereotyped groups—African Americans, overweight people, lawyers, Asians, middle-aged white executives—and list the attributes of that group. As soon as I explained the instructions, the room temperature dropped three degrees. A hand went up and one portfolio manager said,

"How does this help? I mean, how does doing this negative activity lead to anything positive?" The mercury dropped another two degrees.

"Yes, I agree," said a female bond manager, "I don't think this is going to accomplish anything." Cooler still. Almost immediately, several other participants chimed in with similar concerns.

I waited for the other side of the argument to surface, as it always does. Sure enough, a female secretary raised her hand and said, "I took a course on diversity at Oakton Community College last semester, and we did an exercise just like this. It turned out to be very useful."

I waited to see how the detractors would handle her comment. After all, it's hard to refute someone who has actually done the exercise and benefited from it. That testimony tends to carry more weight than people who are merely finding fancy ways to say, "This makes me uncomfortable, so I'd rather not do it."

The secretary's comment hung in the air for a moment, and then the bond woman said: "I don't mean to be insulting but . . . *Oakton Community* College?" She looked around the room for support from her fellow dissenters. "I'm not sure we should draw too many conclusions from a course at a community college."

Needless to say, the secretary was flabbergasted at that remark, as was I. In one breathtaking moment, the bond woman had proven the point beyond any doubt: We all need to examine our prejudices, so they don't embarrass us when we least expect it.

My point in telling this story is to show what an unsafe environment looks like. The secretary stated her opinion, without attacking the other side, and was met with a painful personal assault about her choice of educational establishments. How likely is it that this secretary will feel free to share other personal opinions and feelings that run counter to the group's conscience? The phrase "cold day in hell" comes to mind.

Comparing this diversity experience with safer ones is instructive. The safe groups encourage participants to share their personal truths. The emphasis is on honesty and acceptance. Participants are encouraged to make "I" statements, from their own experience, rather than "we" or "you" statements. (When you use a lot of "you" statements, eventually you don't know whether you means you or I. Confusing, isn't it?)

Confidentiality is important to feeling safe. This turned out to be another sticking point in the investment diversity experience. When asked if the group would respect the confidentiality of the discussion, a lawyer (bless his litigious heart) said, "You can't guarantee anything here. None of these agreements are legally binding."

When I asked him what he meant by that comment, he said, "I don't assume for one second that what I say in this room is going to stay here. So it's pointless to have a confidentiality agreement. There is no way to enforce it."

Do you think his comment warmed or chilled the room? Can you say "ice water?" People wrapped themselves a little tighter in their armor. Am I saying that people should never be on guard? Not at all. There are a million situations in life where one needs to be protective and wary. My point is that the level of creativity will vary proportionately with the feeling of safety that exists. Trust and respect are important—and not just in personal growth groups. It is critical to competitive teams as well. The fiercest competition of all takes place in professional sports. (Well, except for parking spaces during the holidays.) Nevertheless, Phil Jackson, ex-coach of the Chicago Bulls and six-time world champion, in *Sacred Hoops* (Hyperion 1995), recommends the same principles that I am suggesting for effective brainstorming:

> Another important aspect of what we do is to create a supportive environment for the players where they feel secure and free from constant scrutiny . . . . In order to build trust, the players need to know that they can be open and honest with each other, without seeing their words in the paper the next day.

Groups that ignore this advice will suffer. I remember a brainstorming meeting for a major life insurance company, in which a new vice president (new from another company) offered a novel suggestion. She said, "Why not send the beneficiary families of the recently deceased insured a live plant to commemorate the person's life and to symbolize that life goes on?" I thought it was an interesting suggestion, but the roomful of "seasoned" executives howled at it. They tore it apart, beat it, kicked it, stomped it, mocked it, and just generally lynched it before they moved on. The VP obviously felt assaulted. But it didn't end there. From that point on in the meeting, whenever a new or unusual idea was suggested, there was a chorus of "Oh sure, and let's send a live plant, too!" Followed, of course, by knee-slapping and convulsive laughter.

I had never seen anything quite like this in a brainstorming session. It was early in my career, and I had no experience or authority to intervene, so I just observed in horror. But it didn't end there, either. In subsequent meetings around the company, whenever anyone brought up a new, unusual idea, the suggestion was met with a chorus of "Send a live green plant!" This VP's suggestion became part of the culture of the company, in a very demeaning way.

Now, here's the punch line (which in this case is delicious). In her previous job, the new VP had worked at a smaller life insurance company, where they had enjoyed tremendous success with the plant strategy. This, of course, is why she mentioned it in the first place! (One of the best strategies for successful creation is to borrow best practices that have worked elsewhere.) The epilogue of this story is that the woman moved on to a career at another company. Was it the plant incident that drove her out? Probably not entirely. In fact, she has a remarkably resilient attitude. But I'll bet it factored in, and I know that it affected her willingness to open the creative spigot and let the ideas flow.

Creating safety is a process that requires careful attention and constant maintenance. One organization that knows a lot about safety is the Mankind Project. They conduct experiential weekends for men (there is a sister organization for women). They allow the participants to explore and often resolve important life issues in a safe setting. The weekend is open to men from all walks of life, religions, sexual orientations, ethnicities, and races. The effects of the weekend are dramatic. I have heard graduates say that their experience was as powerful as the day that their first child was born. Robert Moore—renowned Jungian analyst, author, and graduate of the weekend—believes that it is the best initiatory experience available to men in our country today. (The Mankind Project is now international, with centers in Britain, Canada, and Germany, and has plans for others as well.)

How does the Mankind Project organization create such powerful personal experiences? By creating a safe container, one in which men can wrestle intensely with life issues, knowing that supportive and skillful allies surround them. In the two dozen or so weekends that I've staffed, I've seen countless examples of what I call "everyday" heroes, but one in particular sticks with me.

Bruce was a husband, father, lawyer, and ex-Marine. He was the "toughest" guy participating in the weekend. I like to watch what happens with the toughest guy, because he measures the safety of the container. If he opens up, then the container has met its toughest challenge. If he skates through the weekend relatively unaffected, then the container failed. It wasn't strong enough for him to trust it.

Bruce went through the coldest weekend on record, in the dead of winter in Chicago: zero degrees with a wind chill of minus 30. Mild-mannered, but with a steely look in his eyes, Bruce waited until all the other men had told their stories and wrestled with their personal demons before he spoke. Then, at about midnight in an old camp recreation center, under a full moon, he told us about his experience as a Marine. He said that he had been the last initiate to crack during boot camp. Weeks after each of the others had fallen apart, wept, screamed for their mamas, puked, and begged to go home, Bruce was still taking the punishment. The drill sergeants told stories about him, as they continued to up the ante. Each time they turned up the heat, Bruce responded with more internal strength.

This same internal strength later saved Bruce's life when his helicopter was hit by enemy fire and crashed over Cambodia. His crew members were all killed, but Bruce managed to jump clear of the crash, falling about 30 feet and breaking both legs as he landed. Refusing to give up, he crawled for three days through the desert with a dislocated eye, broken jaw, and numerous other injuries. Once he got back to the base, he spent nearly six months in the hospital in traction.

When Bruce had finished his story, the room full of 60 men was so quiet you could hear the wind outside. This humble and soft-spoken man had won everyone's respect. But his work still lay ahead. Despite his grim resolve to bear any pain, Bruce had not revealed what he wanted for himself. His face seemed to say, "I'm damned, there is no redemption for me. I must simply carry this burden." Over the next hour, we worked with Bruce to explore his ache. Though respectful of the men who had earlier shared their struggles, Bruce kept repeating his belief that "breaking him down" wouldn't help. "Do you want to see me cry?" he said quietly to the circle of men. "Is that what you want? I don't see how that will help." He still operated from the military paradigm of break them down, humiliate them, and then rebuild them. We respected his concerns and told him that this work was for his own benefit, no one else's. He could stop anytime he wanted. What was painfully clear, though, was that nothing had "shifted" for Bruce. He was stuck. He was just as burdened now as when he arrived on Friday night. His attitude toward the other men was admirable; he was genuinely glad for their breakthroughs and transformations. He just didn't see any path for himself. I remember thinking, "This time we failed, the container wasn't strong enough. He's not going to trust it enough to reach down and exorcise his demon."

But I was wrong. One of the weekend leaders, an ex-military man himself, nicknamed "Alpha Wolf," took charge of the facilitation. He masterfully guided Bruce through a process of grief, forgiveness, and acceptance. Alpha Wolf created a container that was safe enough for Bruce to reveal a Vietnam experience that he had never before confided to anyone. It seems that one of the charming tasks he had been assigned during the war was to assess the condition of wounded villagers. He walked among the writhing, groaning bodies trying to help where he could. Many of them were so badly injured that there was no hope for recovery. Bruce knew this and they did, too. He found himself looking into the eyes of people who begged him to put an end to their misery. In this sense, they were asking him to play the role of God. In an attempt to be merciful, Bruce had many times placed his gun against the temple of a villager and pulled the trigger.

My point in telling this grisly tale is not to shock or depress you, but rather to emphasize the importance of safety. Bruce revealed this nightmare only because he felt safe and was assured that the people in the room had his best interests at heart. Safety is the prerequisite for healing, just as it is the prerequisite for radical creativity. The Mankind Project leaders have studied the process of creating safety and do it as well as anyone.

How?

By creating a sacred space in which people can reveal their whole selves: all the shining virtues and all the character flaws. This same model is used by 12-step recovery groups as well. The principle is simple in theory but extraordinarily difficult in practice, and with good reason. All of us have felt the sting of betrayal. Someone we trusted revealed our secret. Someone used our vulnerability against us. Very quickly, we get smart and learn to set up boundaries—and we keep those barriers in place until our instinct and intelligence agree that it is safe to lower them. (Notice I said "lower," not drop altogether.)

This process requires time, patience, acceptance, courage, and a willingness to let trust develop. The Mankind Project leaders are good at modeling and teaching it. The method is not unlike the age-old kids' dare: I'll show you mine if you'll show me yours. This way people learn over time that it is safe to reveal themselves to the group, because they are assured that it really is safe.

Of all the techniques, tips, and tricks that I have seen or read about for enhancing group creativity, this is the most powerful: creating a safe place. There is nothing like unconditional acceptance for opening the spigot of fresh thinking. Our minds and spirits become like puppies, wildly and ecstatically sniffing and chewing on each new idea, thrilled with the whole experience. At the same time, we become more able to relax, let go of the busyness, and quiet the mind.

So how does a group create a safe place? Learn from an expert. Find someone, your own Alpha Wolf, who has the temperament, skills, experience, and integrity. Why? Because safety has to be modeled. Leaders will lead the way. Typically no group member will go any deeper than the leader is willing to go. Carl Jung noted this fact in his autobiography, *Memories, Dreams, and Reflections* (Vintage 1989). When discussing his own willingness to reveal his weaknesses and character flaws, he said, "I could not expect of my patients something I did not dare to do myself."

Like Jung, leaders who are able to create a safe environment for creativity didn't learn that skill by reading a book, or attending a weekend seminar, or listening to an audiotape while driving. They have had the courage to do their own soul work, day after day, year after year. It is a lifetime commitment to being trustworthy.

The organizations that I have mentioned so far—12-step recovery groups, the Mankind Project, and Interaction Associates—are experts in creating safe environments. In Chapter 17, we'll examine some of the guidelines and exercises that they use to create safe places for brainstorming. In the meantime, here are two sample exercises to get you started.

EXERCISES: CREATING A SAFE PLACE

An exercise that helps create safety involves talking about personal heroes. When I deliver workshops on creativity, I start the day with a round of introductions that includes the question, "Who is a creative hero [or "shero"] of yours?" Sometimes I will explain a brainstorming tool like mindmapping first and let the participants use it to collect their thoughts about their heroes. In any case, I will ask participants to stand, give their name, role, and some other basics and then talk about their creative hero. The choices range from mothers to fathers, children, favorite teachers, spouses, current and former bosses, and some unusual ones like music or nature. The latter are cited as inspiration for creativity. In one workshop, an African-American man with a stutter told us that his mother had been a creative inspiration to him. Why? Because each Christmas, despite the family's poverty, she had managed to create wonderful homemade gifts for each of the nine children. In his words, she had performed magic, something from nothing. And that was his definition of creativity: the ability to produce something from thin air. Another man, neatly dressed, from the accounting department, told the group that his hero was Jesus Christ, who was creating all things anew, to quote the New Testament. This man saw the essence of creativity as the ability to continually bring new things into being.

The beauty of this exercise, I've found, is that it asks people to be revealing in a safe and positive way. Newly formed groups aren't ready to have members reveal their most embarrassing moment. The creative-hero exercise is an effective way to get participants to "go deep" and reveal some of their passion almost immediately after the workshop begins. With a dozen participants, the exercise will take nearly half an hour, so it is time-consuming. But because I believe that safety is the number one contributor to creativity, I take the time. At the end of the workshop, participants often mention that opening exercise and comment positively about it. They say that it set the tone for the rest of the day.

There's another exercise that Interaction Associates uses successfully in the corporate setting when they want to "warm up" the room. Used in conjunction with vision work (i.e., creating inspiring visions for their teams), participants are asked to bring an object from their desks or one that is on their person that has special personal value to them. Usually people bring family pictures, religious icons, or cherished objects like a grandfather's watch or a child's lock of hair. When given the opportunity to talk about the things that have special meaning in their lives, the participants come alive, and the room really does warm up. People feel more connected. The visions that participants craft are always richer and deeper because the participants have tapped into their hearts and remembered what is truly important to them.

CHAPTER 17

Guidelines for Safety

Any fool can criticize, condemn, and complain—and most fools do.

—Dale Carnegie

Let's assume that your group has one or more members who can model safety. What guidelines do the experts use? Of course, these experts are interested in safety for purposes different from ours, such as productive meetings and personal growth. Nevertheless, the guidelines apply to our interest as well: accessing creativity.

The Mankind Project hands out a list of "Rules and Guidelines" to every new group that is formed. They are as follows:

Rules:

1. Take responsibility for yourself.
2. Tell the truth.
3. What you hear here and who you see here stays here. Respect the confidentiality of others.

Guidelines:

1. Speak freely and openly. You need not ask permission to speak, intervene, move around, or contribute in any fashion. However, it is easier if only one person speaks at a time.

2. Speak directly to another person. Instead of saying, "John seems to be angry," speak directly to him: "John, you seem to be angry."

3. Any person may "pass." If anyone is uncomfortable with an exercise or topic, he has the right not to participate. This needs to be honored by group leaders as well as group members.

4. Be aware of feelings. Try to express them because avoidance of feelings is so ingrained in our culture. Encourage feeling statements like "I feel happy." (Rather than, "I'm okay." The word "okay" is not a feeling.)

5. Be here now. Emphasize the present.

6. Use "I" statements. Rather than using the editorial "we" or "you," speak for yourself: "I feel confident."

Twelve-step groups follow similar guidelines, with one notable exception: They prohibit cross-talk. That is, when one person is speaking, all others just listen, without giving feedback either during or after the comments. This practice helps to create safety in the group by eliminating even the possibility of judgment. (In fact, I've been in meetings where even body language was discouraged: nodding, frowning, and so on.) Most people who attend 12-step-style meetings love this aspect of the experience, because they get to tell their story without being judged. The more common experience, especially with men, is that we tell our story and then get deluged with advice like the losing football coach on the sidelines. The contrast in 12-step groups feels almost sacred: a roomful of people listening without formulating responses or designing fixes for you.

Another reason why 12-step meetings prohibit cross-talk is because they are leaderless meetings. If controversy or conflict arose in the process of giving feedback, no one would be authorized to step in and facilitate a resolution.

If you want to experiment with how difficult it is for groups simply to listen and not give advice, try an exercise called an "Inquiry Circle." It's really very simple. One person with an issue sits in the middle of the group. He states his issue, for example: "I want to get out of the office and visit more companies." Next he contracts with the group to define their role. (They are not there to fix his problem.) In this case, he might contract with them to help him get a clearer idea of why he's not seeing more companies. The questioning begins, following these simple rules:

1. The same person cannot ask two questions in a row.
2. All questions must be related to the prior one.
3. All questions should be open-ended (not "yes" or "no" answers).

An opening question might be, "Tell us about your travel patterns now."

To which the man might respond, "I'm traveling about once per month, seeing about two companies."

Next question (from different person): "Have you attended many industry conferences?"

Facilitator: "DING! You've just asked a leading question. Your question implies an answer: If you went to more conferences, you could see more companies. The point of this inquiry exercise is to avoid subtle suggestions for solutions and instead truly inquire into the person's thinking."

When safety is an issue, as in brainstorming, a circle is often the ideal arrangement of chairs or seating. The circle is a symbol of equality. Everyone can see everyone else, and there is no power difference, such as implied by the "head" of the table.

Groups that are interested in establishing safety usually start a meeting with some sort of check-in, a ritual that allows members to get "present," to leave the stresses of the day behind—and, importantly, to leave as many judgments as possible from the day behind. The Mankind Project uses a nice formula: PIE. This acronym stands for:

P: Physical

I: Intellectual

E: Emotional

People comment briefly on each area of their lives. In a new group, the leader may go first to model it for others:

> I'm Joe Bloe. Physically, I'm feeling tired, I've had a long day. My back hurts and my throat is scratchy. Intellectually, I feel pretty clear. I've been reading a great book on Websites that really is fascinating. Emotionally, I feel nervous, since I don't know some of you men. And since I'm the leader I feel some performance anxiety. Like I'm supposed to do everything just right. Even though I know that there isn't a "right way to do this. But I also feel excited about the start of this group. I'm in.

When the speaker finishes—and says "I'm in"—he usually feels more present in the room and less scattered. As others reveal their doubts and limitations, the room becomes safer to simply be real. And from that realness comes the willingness to risk and stretch creatively.

An example of this occurred for me in a writer's workshop in Taos, New Mexico. The leader, Natalie Goldberg (author of *Writing Down the Bones*, Bantam 1988) is excellent at creating safe places. She reads her own blemished, unedited writing exercises right along with the rest of the participants. She is one of the most "real" people you could ever hope to meet. One of the attendees was a professional writer with the *New York Times*. Sidney's first writing attempts at the workshop were full of clever, intellectual puns and references that showed the rest of us his brilliance. They were the work of a "professional" writer.

Three days later Sidney's writing was transformed. He had listened to a woman's writing about her experience as a prostitute and another's description of her rape attack. He had witnessed the power of mutual trust and respect. Safety. He finally felt safe enough to descend into his own deeper creativity. His truth. Sidney wrote in simple, heart-rending language about his attempt to gain his father's approval. I wish I could quote the passage here, because it was so powerful that everyone in the room, including Natalie, was moved to tears. Everyone knew that Sidney had touched on a whole new part of his soul and creativity. He was writing with real passion and guts, not playing it safe to please or impress others. Paradoxically, by dropping his strategy for writing clever material to please people, he actually did much more than please them. He wowed them.

Another tool for creating safety is the physical environment itself. One of the best spaces in this regard is called the Thinkubator, run by Gerald Haman, nicknamed by clients "Solutionman." Gerald has created a terrific working space in his extensive Chicago loft, which features wood floors, large windows with a view of Chicago's skyline, high ceilings, brightly colored walls, toys and gadgets everywhere, fun furniture (like a red couch shaped like giant lips and beanbag chairs), great food and drinks, and hot coffee. A separate playroom contains games and all the equipment for karaoke: microphones, congas, tambourines, shakers, a CD player (with 200 CDs and all the titles printed out for people to choose their favorite songs), and lyrics that are displayed on a giant screen.

Gerald's clients rave about this comfortable and fun space. It goes beyond suggesting that the inner child come out and play, it begs them to! And clients, like General Electric and General Mills, respond by relaxing and letting the ideas flow. In fact, Gerald's process is so effective that it has even attracted an investment firm as a client. (As noted in an earlier chapter, I have yet to learn of an investment firm that has hired an expert to help with brainstorming. Perhaps this firm's success will encourage others to try.)

Is this hoopla really effective, though? Don't executives in typical meeting rooms come up with just as many good ideas? Not according to Dr. Arthur Van Gundy, a professor at the University of Oklahoma. He studied groups that used typical meeting rooms and groups that were treated to a setting like the Thinkubator. His findings showed that the control group of executives churned out 29 ideas in 45 minutes, whereas the "stimulated" group cranked out more than 300 ideas in the same time period! (See Weintraub, *The Hidden Intelligence*, Butterworth Heinemann 1998.)

Clearly then, any influences that promote safety and playfulness will help groups to be more creative. It's only natural that in places like this we shine more brilliantly than we ever imagined possible. That's why I love the work I do toward creating those places. Given safety and support, people come alive and surprise themselves. To paraphrase Walt Disney, it's fun watching people do the impossible.

The rest of this book discusses ways in which investors can recover the power of their creative thinking. In the Myers-Briggs framework, this means having full access to their intuitive preference. In Gary Brinson's language, it means displaying the talents of the second analyst, the one who could take the data and play with it most fruitfully. In Roger Sperry's framework, it means allowing the right brain to flourish. In Carl Jung's language of archetypes, it means accessing the energy of the magician or wizard. Ultimately, it is the capacity to make something of nothing, to take the ordinary and turn it into the extraordinary, to work everyday miracles. For investors, it is the capacity to look at commonly available information and see something different—something significant that will give a competitive edge.

Seven different ideas are presented as guidelines for enhancing your investment thinking. The approach in each case is to introduce the general concept, explain its rationale, and then cite how it has been used successfully in the investment arena. Another way to state this fairly simple approach is: What? So What? Now What?

The most important part for the reader is the final one: Now What? Readers are encouraged to wrestle with each concept and see how it could be applied in their own investing. In workshops, I invariably have to push the participants to make this bridge between the general idea and how they could use it personally. This is the creative step. It will require effort. If you choose not to do it, we will find out who you are and come to your house. No, just kidding. It's true, though, that those who make this extra effort will be rewarded with results. Just as lifting a bar with weights on it is tougher than lifting the bar by itself, so taking this final step is harder. But in each case there is a payoff for the extra effort.

We encourage readers to use any or all of these ideas. There is no formula or process for doing so, but there is an acronym that may help you to remember all seven, if you care: ACROBAT. This word was chosen because it suggests that successful investors in the future will be flexible, able to bend and roll with the rapid changes.

EXERCISE

When I'm working on new ideas, it helps to reread the following quotations and meditate on them.

> "All the durable truths that have come into the world within historic times have been opposed as bitterly as if they were so many waves of smallpox, and every individual who has welcomed and advocated them, absolutely without exception, has been denounced and punished as an enemy of the race." (H. L. Mencken)
>
> "All great Truths begin as blasphemies." (George Bernard Shaw)

I try to really understand and believe that a breakthrough idea will seem absurd. People will laugh at it. They will dismiss it. They may try to "help" you discard it by showing you how it will ruin your career. Or they may be threatened by it simply because it's new, and therefore, well, DIFFERENT! (Like that in itself is bad.) In short, you will run a risk.

So, let me present a half-baked idea that I've been toying with. Perhaps it will encourage you to run with an idea of your own.

I started with the idea that diversification in portfolios is good. Most investors understand and use this principle. Then I played with that idea a little, turning it this way and that. For example, what *kind* of diversification? Geographic? Okay. Market size? All right. Industry exposure? Sure. Most portfolio managers would agree that you don't want to be too lopsided with any of these factors, unless, of course, that's your strategy (for instance, if you want to invest only in small-cap stocks). Fine.

Short of making a conscious bet on some factor, most managers try to balance out their portfolios.

Then, I thought, is there an area where this principle doesn't hold? Where all managers are loading up on a certain factor without offsetting it? Twenty years ago, one could have said, yes, all the companies in most portfolios are run by white, middle-aged males. Therefore, that factor is not being diversified; it's constant throughout. (Today, the diversity funds mentioned elsewhere in this book are addressing this issue.)

How about another factor? Can you think of one that is currently undiversified in today's portfolios? The one that jumps out for me, given my interests, is personality types. Companies—or portfolios—that aren't balanced in this regard will suffer in the marketplace. For example, I've been working with a distribution company that has a good mix of lions, owls, and dolphins, but no foxes. That's a problem because foxes are natural salespeople. They are the ones who make it happen. Another company that I consult with is lousy with lions at the top, even though they are in a business that requires radical change. Not a good outlook, I'd say. This concept of balancing the types within a company or portfolio makes sense to me. But can you imagine what a risk it would be to implement with client money!?

On the lighter side, I've been playing around with another factor: intelligence. Most Wall Street money managers jam their portfolios full of companies that are run by the best and the brightest: graduate degrees from top universities, sizzling IQ scores, Mensa members, and so on. All this despite Peter Lynch's warning that "you should buy stocks of companies that any fool could run, because eventually one will." Well, what about diversifying into the companies run by the duller crayons? The managers who *are* looking for toast in the bread aisle? Meantime, some readers' reaction is, "Okay, but how would you identify the companies with the not-so-bright management?" Herewith I offer Exhibit A identifying my top 10 candidates for the Dumb and Dumber portfolio (these labels were found on actual products on the store shelves):

10. On some **Swanson** frozen dinners: *Serving suggestion: Defrost.*
9. On an **American Airlines** packet of nuts: *Instructions: open packet, eat nuts.*
8. On a bag of **Fritos**: *You could be a winner! No purchase necessary. Details inside.*
7. On a bar of **Dial** soap: *Directions: Use like regular soap.*
6. On a **Sears** hair dryer: *Do not use while sleeping.*
5. On **Tesco's** tiramisu dessert package (printed on the bottom): *Do not turn upside down.*
4. On **Marks & Spencer** bread pudding: *Product will be hot after heating.*
3. On **Boot's Children's** cough medicine: *Do not drive car or operate machinery.*
2. On packaging for a **Rowenta** iron: *Do not iron clothes on body.*
1. On **Nytol** sleep aid: *Warning: may cause drowsiness.*

Any questions?

TOOLS FOR ENHANCING CREATIVITY: "ACROBAT"

The next seven chapters provide guidelines for enhancing your creativity as an investor or as a team of investors. Each chapter title includes a slogan for remembering the guideline. For example, Chapter 18 is called "A is for Assume Nothing." Taken together, the seven chapters spell out the word ACROBAT. Hopefully, these guidelines will limber up your thinking and allow you to navigate gracefully through the market challenges ahead.

CHAPTER 18

"A" Is for Assume Nothing

If you consider yourself a leader at any level of your organization, one of the most valuable activities you can engage in is conversation about the assumptions that underlie the structures and flow of information within that organization, the assumptions that drive all strategies, planning, and decision making activities.

—Glenna Gerard, author of *Dialogue*
(John Wiley & Sons 1998)

Assume nothing. Zero. Bupkus. Zen mind, beginner's mind. This is a touchy subject when it comes to professional investors. We tend to pride ourselves on our knowledge. In fact, in my experience, working with lots of different groups and people from all walks of life, investors may be the world-class know-it-alls. Yes, lawyers and doctors are in the race as well, but professional investors just may take the prize in this area. Painful, self-effacing modesty is not a personal demon that we wrestle with. Personality type explains some of our confidence. All of these professions are loaded with STJ personalities. (STJs are notorious for having the right answers, as the study cited in Chapter 5 indicated.)

In the case of investors, though, much of our self-assurance comes from training. *Training?* Yes. Investors are trained to spot a pig in a poke, to sniff out the bogus deal, to reveal that the little man behind the curtain is a fake. They are pros at it, and in this respect they are great warriors, fighting through sham and illusion to unearth the financial truth, confidently wielding analytical swords.

This combination of personality type and training can be deadly, though.

All strengths have corresponding weaknesses, and the downside of the investor's natural skepticism is that it kills creativity. These samurai rarely put their swords down long enough to be playfully innocent. Being competent is a deep core value to many investment pros, so the idea of dropping their certainty and assuming nothing rubs all their fur and feathers the wrong way. The mere suggestion of exposing their ignorance is about as much fun as optical surgery with a butter knife.

The behavioral finance folks have researched this phenomenon and named it. They call it "overconfidence." (For once, psychologists came up with a name that Ockham would have loved.) The evidence for overconfidence is the sort that appeals to the strength of investors: analytic reasoning. Investors will listen to and quite possibly accept this sort of evidence as a reason to change. (We all know that the only people who like change are panhandlers and wet babies.) One of the leading figures in the field of behavioral finance, Amos Tversky, said that investors "are generally overconfident. They acquire too much confidence from the information that is available to them, and they think they are right much more often than they actually are" (*Behavioral Finance and Decision Theory in Investment Management*, AIMR Publications 1995). This sort of overconfidence results in famous bloopers like the ones listed earlier ("heavier-than-air flying machines are impossible," etc.). These statements remind us that "the true obstacle to progress is not ignorance but the illusion of knowledge," to quote Daniel Boorstin of the Library of Congress. If you don't believe that you are overconfident, try the quiz at the end of this chapter.

Evidence for overconfident behavior comes from many fields.

In one study of the medical field, doctors were asked to diagnose which patients had pneumonia. The doctors were told to select only the cases where they were 90 percent sure of the diagnosis. After the doctors completed their exams and diagnoses, follow-up studies showed that only 50 percent of the patients selected actually had pneumonia.

It's no better in the investment arena. In one study, analysts were asked to specify a trading range for a given stock. (This was before the days of dot.com stocks, when a reasonable range would be, say, $5 to $500 for a given week.) Like the doctors in the earlier study, the analysts were told to be 90 percent sure that they were right about the range. In this case, the analysts did a little better than the doctors. One could have expected about 10 percent of the stocks to violate the rule and move outside the range, but in fact 35 percent of the stocks traded outside it. The conclusion? Again, overconfidence. We think we know more than we actually do. (Does this ever happen to you? You are at a party and someone asks what band recorded "Wooly Bully." No one knows—but you do. You are absolutely certain that it was The McCoys, so you clear your throat modestly and enlighten everyone. Oh, it's so great. You are Mr./Ms. Know-it-all. That is, until some smarty-pants surfs the Net on his Palm Pilot and announces, "No, it was Sam the Sham and the Pharaohs." Damn. I hate that.)

In the face of our rampant overconfidence, one of the best ego deflators in the investment world is Mark Hulbert, publisher of the *Hulbert Financial Digest.* He runs many rigorous statistical tests to see which investment newsletters are demonstrating true expertise in picking stocks and which are just lucky. Of the newsletters that he follows, 89 have been around for 10 years or more. Hulbert subjected the performance of these newsletters to a "runs test" to see if any of the funds could be credited with a hot hand for the period. In fact, three of the newsletters passed the test. Are these the true market savants? Does this mean that we should rush out and subscribe? Although many investors do exactly that, the answer is no. Hulbert explains that in this test you would expect to see four false positives. In other words, by sheer luck, four newsletters should have outperformed. Put another way, if you had 89 coin flippers, four of them would show "expertise" in coin flipping, even though we know that they would simply be experiencing good luck. Hulbert conducted the same study with newsletters that have five-year records and got similar results: 219 newsletters and 10 winners. But the number of false positives was predicted to be 11. What's the conclusion? There is no evidence that any of the newsletters outperforms. Regardless, because of overconfidence, investors chase the latest winner, and marketers play on this behavior mercilessly. They advertise one-year performance numbers with a bullhorn from the tops of buildings. (Finally, their clatter woke up Arthur Levitt at the SEC, and he personally sent out a message warning firms about this practice.)

David Dreman and Michael Berry also studied overconfidence and got similar results. In fact, their study, conducted in 1995, showed that analysts' estimates were actually deteriorating in accuracy! The forecast error for estimates (that is, a prediction of by how much analyst estimates would miss the actual reported earnings) had moved from the 20–30 percent range up to more than 60 percent by 1990.

Dreman also points out in his writings that analysts bolster their already inflated confidence by spending hours on additional research, collecting additional bits of information on companies. Typically this extra digging doesn't improve the investment decision, but it does let the analyst sleep better.

So what's to be done?

The quality of creative thinking can be enhanced only if investors practice letting go of their certainty. After all, thinking is the capacity to hold different points of view, to consider things from all sides, and finally to make a decision. Somehow in this culture, we got it just backward: We consider the smartest people to be the ones who are absolutely certain of their answers and can win any debate by outshouting their opponents. But holding fast to one idea and arguing blindly and vehemently for it is, ironically, not thinking at all.

A good way to practice real thinking is to seek out intelligent people who hold opposite viewpoints. Listen carefully to their arguments, without trying to debate. Get in their shoes. Challenge yourself to understand deeply how an intelligent person could hold this opposite opinion. Use the skills of the sensing and thinking types to objectively dissect the arguments and see exactly where you disagree. This approach takes courage. Most of us don't want to rock the foundation of our belief systems, but this adventure is what creative thinking is all about. Sometimes it makes you sweat.

Much of what we believe to be good thinking comes from our knowledge of high-school debates and television courtrooms. In both cases, there is a competition and a goal: to win. Returning to our discussion of types for a moment, remember that "thinking" types prefer competition, whereas "feeling" types prefer cooperation. Hence, in both the legal and investment fields the dominant form of thinking is a competitive debate. We get ego points for looking smart and making our points.

This ego-stroking behavior was the subject of a study that used *New York Times* theatrical reviews. Participants were asked to read reviews and place them in one of two piles: smart writer or not-so-smart writer. Invariably, the reviews that ended up in the "smart" pile were scathing criticisms, whereas the "not-so-smart" pile was filled with complimentary reviews. The trick to the study was that *all* the reviews had actually been written by the same person—showing that we tend to view critical thinking as smarter than complimentary thinking. Our culture definitely favors the debating model. It strokes our egos. We get rewarded for being critical.

However, the really creative investors must be skillful in both types of reasoning. They can debate when appropriate *and* they can undertake dialogue about subjects when the goal is new ideas and different mental models. The art of dialogue—the kind that physicist David Bohm and Fifth Discipline guru Peter Senge write about—is not a simple process. It requires skill and commitment and, perhaps most importantly, humility.

Does humility help? Apparently so. In their book, *Decision Traps* (Simon & Schuster 1989), authors Russo and Schoemaker report that Jay Freedman, a top investment analyst with Kidder, Peabody and Company, credits them with helping him to overcome his overconfidence. Rather than falling into the typical know-it-all trap, Freedman

> deliberately asks questions designed to "disconfirm" what he thinks is true. If Freedman thinks the disposable diaper business is becoming less price competitive, for example, he will ask executives a question that implies the opposite such as, "Is it true that price competition is getting tougher in disposable diapers?" This kind of question makes him more likely than competing analysts to get the real story, and Freedman's "buy" recommendations have consistently added value for his clients.

Assume nothing. Much easier said than done.

EXERCISE 1: OVERCONFIDENCE QUIZ

Don't believe that you are overconfident? Try this quiz. Developed by J. Edward Russo and Paul H. Schoemaker, each of these questions calls for a numerical answer. Record your answer in a "best guess" column. On either side of that number, put a higher and lower guess that you are quite sure contains the correct answer.

For example, if the question is "How much did the S&P 500 increase in 1999?" you might guess 15 percent. Then you might pick 10 percent and 20 percent as the bottom and top limits. You believe with 90 percent confidence that the correct answer will be between 10 percent and 20 percent. (The correct answer is 19.5 percent, so you would be within the 90 percent confidence interval.)

1. How much did the NASDAQ stock market increase in 1999?
2. How long is the Nile River?
3. How many words are there in the English language?
4. When was Genghis Khan born?
5. How many miles long is the Great Wall of China?
6. What is the population of Pakistan?
7. What is the distance in miles between Pluto and our sun?
8. What was the gross domestic product of Brazil in 1994?
9. How many employees did Mobil Corporation have in 1998?
10. When was Harvard University founded?

Compare your ranges with the correct answers, given at the end of this exercise, and see how many answers fell outside the range that you specified. If you are like 99 percent of the executives who have taken tests like this, you had more than one answer that was outside the range. In fact, most executives had six or more fall outside the range! See what we mean about overconfidence?

Answers: 1) 85.6 percent; 2) 4,187 miles; 3) 730,000; 4) A.D. 1167; 5) 1,500; 6) 129,270,000; 7) 3.67 billion; 8) $640 billion; 9) 43,000; 10) A.D. 1636. (*Sources*: Microsoft's *Encarta* encyclopedia; *Wall Street Journal*.)

EXERCISE 2: CLEAN SLATE

On a plain sheet of paper, write down your beliefs about the investment world. What ideas are you absolutely certain of? Are you certain that diversification is good? Are you positive that earnings growth is the most important factor in stock prices? Are you sure that risk and return are always correlated (more risk is the only way to get more return)?

Whatever they are, list your beliefs on your paper.

Now, imagine wiping the slate clean. What new ideas and strategies could you experiment with if you dropped these beliefs? Find intelligent people who don't hold these beliefs, and seek to understand their position. Lessen your certainty. Approach investing from an attitude of openness.

CHAPTER 19

"C" Is for Change Gears

Genius is eternal patience.
> —Michelangelo

Patience is a necessary ingredient of genius.
> —Benjamin Disraeli

Change gears. Some of us get our best ideas while driving or jogging or showering. Albert Einstein used to wonder why he got his niftiest thoughts while shaving. One woman in a workshop said that she got her best ideas while walking in circles around a conference room and talking out loud, periodically stopping to jot something on a flip chart. Hey, whatever works.

Changing gears refers to moving from the high-paced, focused mode to the slower-paced, flexible mode. The comedian John Cleese, in a short video on creativity, refers to these two modes as "closed" and "open." They are both useful. Left-brainers tend to live in the closed mode, right-brainers in the open. When working on a deadline, the closed mode is ideal. Head down, door closed, no interruptions. The last thing you want when you're in this mode is some "idea" person butting in and saying, "Have you thought about . . . ." Throw a heavy paperweight at them and make a mental note to mail-bomb their PCs—later.

The problem in the fast-paced investment world is that we get stuck in the closed mode. We are always being asked to do more with less. We always have deadlines. The markets are always hectic. The pace is frantic. The mind races—and, as Theodore Roethke said, "A mind too active is no mind at all." The stress levels tend to freeze us in repetitive patterns. Jack Treynor, an original thinker in the investment world, has an opinion on this. Jack notes about our habitual behavior that "patterns in the way active managers manage tend to become grooves—irrespective of their merits" ("Zero Sum," *Financial Analyst Journal*, Jan./Feb. 1994). In other words, investors get stuck in ruts. Art Zeikel, formerly of Merrill Lynch, makes a similar point in an article in the *Financial Analyst Journal* ("Organizing for Creativity," Nov./Dec. 1983). He says that professional investors go to the same schools, read the same books and reports, and follow the same valuation guidelines, so it's no wonder that they tend to reach the same conclusions—and tend to get the same mediocre results.

How do we as investors learn to change gears? How do we train ourselves to tap into the benefits of the open mode?

As with most change, the first step is awareness. We need to understand that there are two modes, and we need to be aware of the importance of the open mode. Edward Jenner never would have discovered the vaccine for smallpox if he had focused only on sick people. His research with them was getting him nowhere. Fortunately, he was able to shift to the open mode and notice that dairy maids never contracted smallpox. This led him to the hypothesis that they were somehow protected against the disease. In fact, most of them had contracted the harmless cowpox, which then conferred immunity from the deadly smallpox.

Jenner's success resulted from his capacity to try something different. He did not endlessly repeat an unsuccessful pattern. He interrupted it and tried a new and—as it turned out—successful approach. In our high-speed world, it is increasingly difficult to slow down and see things anew. Einstein himself said that he wasn't necessarily smarter than other people; rather, he gave himself the chance to study a problem for a long time. In following his fascination, he went deeply into the problem and eventually saw it differently. This ability to slow down and follow our bliss, as Joseph Campbell used to say, is critical to creative thought. B.F. Skinner expresses it this way: "When you find something interesting, drop everything else and study it. Too many fail to answer opportunity's knock at the door because they have to finish some preconceived plan" (quoted in Michalko, *Cracking Creativity*, Ten Speed Press 1998).

The open mode has a different feel. Stand and stretch for a moment, let your thoughts wander. (In the church that I attend, the minister always starts his sermon with a moment of silence. He reminds us that for the next 60 seconds, "There is no place to go, nothing to do, no one we have to be.") This feeling of openness is close to that of children at play. Their only purpose is fun and discovery. They don't have a particular goal in mind. As creative investors, we need to give ourselves permission to do the same. We need to be okay with finding a quiet place to think.

One of the most successful investors I know is Roger Brown. He used to run Harris Associates, where Ralph Wanger's Acorn Fund was born (planted?). When I think of what makes Roger successful, it goes back to the eight great traits. He has and exercises all of them. In particular, though, he gives himself plenty of time to think. When I visit him and his family, I usually find that he has been reading and thinking. He is dressed in something comfortable, like corduroys and a wooly sweater. He always peppers me with a barrage of questions, clearly ones that were floating through his mind just moments before. My point is that he allows himself time to slow down and think. He enjoys it. It's his hobby. (Though, like Warren Buffett, he's learned to live with the sizeable proceeds.) I once asked Roger why he didn't index everything, à la Jack Bogle, and his response was, "I'd get bored." Investing, and more specifically, thinking, is his passion.

Simple as it sounds, one key to higher creativity is slowing down. The consulting group that I mentioned earlier, Interaction Associates, has a slogan, "Go slow to go fast." At first I thought it sounded a little corny, but I have seen it work repeatedly in the past few years. Perhaps one of the reasons that analyst earnings estimates are deteriorating, as noted in the last chapter, is precisely this issue of speed. As they race to cover stocks and grab banking deals, the quality of their thinking suffers.

Slowing down is a matter of awareness. It's knowing when you are in the closed, focused mode and when you are open and receptive. Many of the great discoveries in the history of thought are the result of this subtle difference. Penicillin, sticky notes, smallpox vaccine: all were accidents. They resulted from the researcher's being open enough to a perceived failure to reframe it. (The classic case of this is Edison's response that he had not failed to discover the appropriate filament for a light bulb; rather, he had successfully found a thousand filaments that did not work.) This notion that creativity is often accidental is the premise of a book called *Corporate Creativity* (Berrett-Koehler 1997) by Alan Robinson and Sam Stern. The opening story in the book tells how a Japanese railroad company discovered a new business quite by accident. While digging tunnels to lay new tracks, the company stumbled on a reservoir of natural water. It tasted so good that they began bottling it and eventually marketing it. Within a few years, bottled water was a multimillion-dollar business for this railroad company. Why? Because they were in the open mode. They were receptive to new ideas and possibilities. Robinson and Stern suggest in their book that this open mode is a powerful tool for creative companies. You can't make creativity happen, but you can train your people to be open to serendipity.

Returning to our discussion of types, the most open types are "intuitives" and "perceivers." They tend to live in the open mode. The most focused types are "sensors" and "judgers." They would be the least likely to look at a "failed" experiment and say,

"Hmmm, maybe this isn't a failure after all. We just need to look at it differently."

A simple personal example may demonstrate the value of slowing down. Soon after I was linked to the Internet, I was asked to make a presentation to the business students at the Kellogg School of Management. As I was preparing the slides on the day of the presentation, I was hit by an inspiration: Why not include the Wildcat mascot on the slides? After all, Northwestern had just gone to the Rose Bowl, a relative rarity, so why not celebrate? Because I was in closed mode—head down, pounding out the work to meet the deadline—I raced to my car, drove three miles to Central Street where a merchant sells NU logos, bought one with the Wildcat on it, and tore home. Once back at my desk, I scanned in the logo, saved it to a file, and then imported it to my Power Point presentation. Total elapsed time: 20 minutes. It was only later (with an audible "Doh" like Homer Simpson's) that I realized I could have gotten the Wildcat logo online from NU's Website. A no-brainer. Go to a search engine, plug in "Northwestern," right-click on the mascot, and hit "Copy." Total elapsed time would have been about two minutes. Savings: a factor of 10. I am convinced that all business everywhere could enjoy these same savings if only they encouraged their people to move in and out of the closed mode, as appropriate.

The true beauty of this suggestion is that it only requires a few minutes each day.

CHAPTER 20

"R" Is for Risking Discomfort

Necessity is the mother of taking chances.
—Mark Twain

"R" is for risking discomfort. Innovators take chances. They push the envelope. They learn to accept the discomfort of creative tension. They're sort of like the fellow whose doctor told him: "You've been under a lot of stress, you need to relax." To which the man replied, "I tried relaxing, but—I don't know—I feel more comfortable tense."

This paradox of being more comfortable while tense is where the creator lives. Unfortunately, many of the messages of our culture emphasize comfort as the goal of life. A variation on the bumper sticker, "The one with the most toys wins" might be "The one with the comfiest La-Z-Boy wins." C.S. Lewis made a good comment on that:

> Comfort is the one thing you cannot get by looking for it. If you look for truth, you may find comfort in the end. If you look for comfort, you will not get either comfort or truth—only soft soap and wishful thinking to begin with and, in the end, despair [*Mere Christianity*, Macmillan 1952].

Workshop participants sometimes resist when I tell them that creativity involves pain. Just like exercise: When all is said and done, you need to put on your sneakers and do it. And, typically, if you're not used to exercise, you'll be sore afterward. What I try to offer clients is a fun, hard workout. Think of it this way: You can get good exercise playing a vigorous game of tennis or walking 18 holes of golf . . . or you could do jumping jacks for 30 minutes. All of these would raise your heart rate and burn off calories. Most people would agree, though, that a game is more enjoyable. My intention is to design creative sessions that are both productive and fun. But sometimes, try as one might, creative projects are just hard work. I often refer to Michelangelo's plaint: "People would not be so awed by my creations if they knew how hard I worked to produce them."

Along these lines, John Cleese gives this advice: Set aside 90 minutes for creative thinking and then assume that the first 30 will be awkward and unpleasant. The trick is knowing that the first part will be tough and preparing for it. It's easier to endure the discomfort if you anticipate it and know that it will ease after about 30 minutes. Too many otherwise creative people never make it through that first circle of fire. They quit after 10 minutes and miss all the good ideas that were waiting just around the next corner. (Some joggers would say that this is similar to "runner's high"; gut it out through the pain and you get a payoff. I wouldn't know. In 20 years of jogging, I've experienced runner's blister, runner's headache, runner's stitch, runner's charlie horse, runner's "quick-where's-the-bathroom?" but never runner's high. Oh, well.)

Another obstacle on the road to full-blown creativity is the temptation to play it safe. No one ever wins by crowding into the center of the herd. Of course, no one who does that ever looks foolish, either.

Investment professionals wrestle with this dilemma every day. It would be easy to put a finger in the wind and discover which stocks are most popular. It would be safe to buy those stocks because, after all, everyone owns them. Another variation on this theme might be to peek at Warren Buffett's holdings or the Janus fund's (they are publicly available, after all) and then duplicate that portfolio. (Isn't it an odd profession that allows you to do this? In grade school this was called *cheating*. In business it's called *best practices*.) This approach of borrowing the best practices of others looks especially attractive when you consider the alternative: daring independence! Mustering your courage and your capacity for radical thought and striking out on your own. Yikes! No thanks, Dilbert and I will wait here in the cubicle.

Again, though, personality style is relevant.

Which types are most likely to accept risk? As noted earlier, the foxes (SPs) like risk. They are the hedge-fund managers and day traders. They love action and adventure. In fact, they would hate copying someone else's portfolio. Typically, then, foxes are already primed for risk taking. They are natural-born contrarians. Index funds? Forget it.

In contrast, lions (SJs) don't like risk. They tend to be tenacious and effective but only with the traditional techniques. They like stability and steadiness. Remember their motto, "I'm steady." They will be most resistant to dramatic contrarian investments.

Having worked in several shops that were heavily stocked with lions, I know this behavior first-hand. One lion chief investment officer continually talked a good game about risky new growth opportunities, like starting a mutual fund, or acquiring one, or spinning off the investment department and making it a separate entity. Bold plans, rife with risk, they conjured up the image of Lewis and Clark or the search for the Northwest Passage. The truth was more like Homer Simpson rooting around in the fridge for a doughnut. Given the lion (SJ) nature of this CIO, each time he drew his sword for a new adventure, he instead used it to cut expenses by selling off asset groups or reducing headcount. Lions tend to be great cost cutters, but growth, especially when it involves significant risks, is very difficult for them. The solution in this case would have been a balance between the SJ lion energy and the NP magician or court jester energy. However, this balance would have required acceptance and skillful management of creative conflict. Lions and jesters typically butt heads, so lions are more comfortable when they are surrounded by other lions, who see the world in the same way. This is exactly what this CIO did: He surrounded himself with other lions. This strategy may be costly, if the premise of this book is correct: namely, that investors will need a balanced approach to succeed in the future. The notion of the Prudent Man must be balanced with that of the Maverick Woman.

Another example of lions and risk aversion comes from my experience in consulting about creativity and change. A major insurance company was redefining its relationship to the customer. They were asking questions like, "Should we just try to sell, sell, sell? Or should we diagnose and prescribe, more like doctors and patients?" The senior management made a wholehearted commitment to examining and shifting paradigms. (Oops, sorry. I used the "P" word. I meant "mental models.") They called in consultants and involved the top officers, nearly 100 of them. Hundreds of hours were spent discussing and debating the current sales and marketing effort and how it could be changed. Specifically, the senior leaders asked for "big ideas." They didn't want tweaks around the edges, they wanted the breakthrough concepts. They even passed out crystal paperweights to all those involved that said, "Big ideas can change the world."

Months later, when the initiative had ended, I asked one of the worker bees who had helped facilitate the process whether any significant changes had occurred. The response? No. Very little had really changed. Why? Because this organization was heavy with lions at the top. The brainstorming ceased and guess what continued? Cost cutting. The knee-jerk response of lions to adversity is to prune the organization.

Note that sometimes cost cutting is exactly the right action. In fact, when the lions first took over this company, they initiated expense reduction and Wall Street loved it. The stock soared. More recently, though, as the market continues to reach new highs, the stock price of this company has lost more than 50 percent of its value. The market recognizes that this company's competitors are not only cutting costs but also taking chances with new strategies for growth. These competitors are selling at twice the multiples.

Richard Pzena, from Sanford Bernstein, provides a good discussion of investors' attitude toward risk. He addresses the problem of contrarian investing and how much courage it takes to really be out of favor in the market. Because being out of favor is so painful, he believes that the market operates efficiently by rewarding people for taking on that pain. In other words, if you buy the market "dogs," the stocks that are cheap because everyone hates them, then you will be rewarded. The stocks will go up and you'll outperform. However, there is usually a period of time—several quarters or more—where you will appear to be an idiot. Even the family dog will wonder if you have meatloaf for brains. As Pzena says of these contrarians, "Sometimes they will feel very lonely. Everyone, their clients, their peers, the press—will question their sanity. Such pressure keeps their ranks thin." Pzena, well aware of the emotional pressure on investors to conform, has helped structure the culture and reward system at Sanford Bernstein to encourage contrarian thinking.

This is why one of my tips—"Ask for help"—involves building the right support system around yourself, to encourage risk taking. But first let's examine a thinking pattern that severely limits breakthrough thinking . . . after a quick exercise to reveal your tolerance for risk.

EXERCISE

How much risk is right? This quick quiz will give you an idea of where you fall on the spectrum.

1. Your investment loses 15 percent of its value in a market correction a month after you buy it. Assuming that none of the fundamentals have changed, do you:
   a) Sit tight and wait for it to journey back up.
   b) Sell it and rid yourself of further sleepless nights if it continues to decline.
   c) Buy more—if it looked good at the original price, it looks even better now.

2. A month after you purchase it, the value of your investment suddenly skyrockets by 40 percent. Assuming you can't find any further information, what do you do?
   a) Sell it.
   b) Hold it on the expectation of further gain.
   c) Buy more—it will probably go higher.

3. Which would you have rather done:
   a) Invested in an aggressive growth fund that appreciated very little in six months.
   b) Invested in a money-market fund only to see the aggressive growth fund you were thinking about double in value in six months.

4. Would you feel better if:
   a) You doubled your money in an equity investment?
   b) Your money-market fund investment saved you from losing half your money in a market slide?

5. Which situation would make you feel happiest?
   a) You win $100,000 in a publisher's contest.
   b) You inherit $100,000 from a rich relative.
   c) You earn $100,000 by risking $2,000 in the options market.
   d) Any of the above—you're happy with the $100,000 no matter how it ended up in your wallet.

6. The apartment building where you live is being converted to condominiums. You can either buy your unit for $80,000 or sell the option for $20,000. The market value of the condo is $120,000. You know that if you buy the condo, it might take six months to sell, the monthly carrying cost is $1,200, and you'd have to borrow the down payment for a mortgage. You don't want to live in the building anymore. What do you do?
   a) Take the $20,000.
   b) Buy the unit and then sell it on the open market.

7. You inherit your uncle's $100,000 house, free of any mortgage. Although the house is in a fashionable neighborhood and can be expected to appreciate at a rate faster than inflation, it has deteriorated badly. It would net $1,000 monthly if rented as is; it would net $1,500 per month if renovated. The renovations could be financed by a mortgage on the property. You would:
   a) Sell the house.
   b) Rent it as is.
   c) Make the necessary renovations, and then rent it.

8. You work for a small, but thriving, privately held electronics company. The company is raising money selling stock to its employees. Management plans to take the company public, but not for four more years. If you buy the stock, you will not be allowed to sell until shares are traded publicly. In the meantime, the stock will pay no dividends. However, when the company goes public, the shares could trade for 10 to 20 times what you paid for them. How much of an investment would you make?
   a) None at all.
   b) One month's salary.
   c) Three months' salary.
   d) Six months' salary.

9. Your longtime friend and neighbor, an experienced petro-
   leum geologist, is assembling a group of investors (of which
   he is one) to fund an exploratory oil well, which could pay
   back 50 to 100 times the investment if successful. If the
   well is dry, the entire investment is worthless. Your friend
   estimates the chance of success at only 20 percent. What
   would you invest?
   a) Nothing at all.
   b) One month's salary.
   c) Three months' salary.
   d) Six months' salary.

10. You learn that several commercial building developers are
    seriously looking at undeveloped land in a certain loca-
    tion. You are offered an option to buy a choice parcel of
    that land. The cost is about 2 months' salary and you
    calculate the gain to be 10 months' salary. Do you:
    a) Purchase the option.
    b) Let it slide; it's not for you.

11. You are on a TV game show and can choose one of the
    following. Which would you take?
    a) $1,000 in cash.
    b) A 50 percent chance at winning $4,000.
    c) A 20 percent chance at winning $10,000.
    d) A 5 percent chance at winning $100,000.

12. It's 2002, and inflation is returning. Hard assets such as
    precious metals, collectibles, and real estate are expected
    to keep pace with inflation. Your assets are now all in long-
    term bonds. What do you do?
    a) Hold the bonds.
    b) Sell the bonds, putting half the proceeds into money
       funds and the other half into hard assets.
    c) Sell the bonds and put the total proceeds into hard as-
       sets.

    d) Sell the bonds, put all the money into hard assets, and borrow additional money to buy more.

13. You've lost $500 at the blackjack table in Atlantic City. How much more are you prepared to lose to win the $500 back?
    a) Nothing—you quit now.
    b) $100.
    c) $250.
    d) $500.
    e) More than $500.

Your score: Now it's time to see what kind of investor you are. Total your score, using the following point system for each answer you gave.

    1. A—3, B—1, C—4
    2. A—1, B—3, C—4
    3. A—1, B—3
    4. A—2, B—1
    5. A—2, B—1, C—4, D—1
    6. A—1, B—2
    7. A—1, B—2, C—3
    8. A—1, B—2, C—4, D—6
    9. A—1, B—3, C—6, D—9
  10. A—3, B—1
  11. A—1, B—3, C—5, D—9
  12. A—1, B—2, C—3, D—4
  13. A—1, B—2, C—4, D—6, E—8

If you scored:

Below 21: You are a conservative investor, allergic to risk. Stay with sober, conservative investments. The tips on creative investing will seem like a real stretch and the risk involved makes you break out in hives. You probably have a "J" in your Myers-Briggs type.

21 to 35: You are an active investor, willing to take calculated, prudent risks to gain financially. You will probably have a "P" in your Myers-Briggs type.

36 or more: You are a venturesome, aggressive investor. You probably have a "P" in your Myers-Briggs type, and very likely an "S" too.*

---

*Reprinted with permission from the author, Bill Donoghue.

CHAPTER 21

"O" Is for Omit
Either/Or Thinking

Evolution always transcends and includes, incorporates and goes beyond.

—Ken Wilber, *A Brief History of Everything*
(Shambala 1996)

Omit "either/or" thinking. This technique for increasing creativity is related to the notion of discomfort in Chapter 20. Our culture thrives on black-and-white solutions. We love movies like *Star Wars* that pit Good against Evil. We like political scenarios that cast the United States in a saintly white glow, while Russia and Iraq are shown in devilish black. We drool over courtroom dramas that have clear decisions. O.J. is innocent and walks. Nixon is guilty and goes down. We like sports with clear winners and sudden-death playoffs in the event of ties.

The technique discussed in this chapter involves a different approach. It involves the ability to hold the tension of the opposites, to accept that discomfort, and to wait until a third possibility emerges. This is the concept of the Hegelian dialectic: two opposing points of view that merge into a synthesis which produces a better solution than either point alone. Steven Covey, in his best-seller *The 7 Habits of Highly Effective People* (Simon & Schuster 1989), emphasizes this same point in the final habit, "Synergy." Covey says, "Buddhism calls this the middle way. Middle in this sense does not mean compromise; it means higher, like the apex of the triangle." The process of achieving this is very different from a debate, where one side wins. Rather, "they communicate back and forth until they come up with a solution they both feel good about. It's better than the solutions either of them originally proposed."

Another powerful thinker, Ken Wilber, recognized by many as one of the brilliant minds of our time, expresses synergy this way: "Evolution always transcends and includes, incorporates and goes beyond." Real progress does not claim that one way is right and the other wrong, but that a higher and better way includes elements of each.

Examples of either/or thinking in the investment world abound. Fundamental analysts and technical analysts go at each other hammer and tongs. Value investors and momentum investors argue like actors in a beer commercials ("tastes great," "less filling"), back and forth. In truth, all of these schools of thought have something to offer.

It's also like this with behavioral finance advocates and efficient market theorists. The former argue that investors are irrational, that they make systematic and predictable mistakes that "rational" people would not make. In opposition, efficient market believers maintain that people are rational and act rationally when it comes to financial decisions.

Who is right?

Are we irrational or rational? Woody Brock, economist and president of Strategic Economic Decisions, Inc., addresses this split in a *Financial Analysts Journal* article (Dec. 1998) that incorporates "both/and" thinking instead of "either/or." He calls the article, appropriately enough, "The Future of Behavioral Finance: A

Synthesis of Disciplines." Exactly the point. In his article, Brock suggests a resolution for the either/or thinking that surrounds the debate between efficient market proponents and behavioral finance theorists. The solution is a synthesis, a combination of these opposing schools of thought. Brock states the principle of resolution this way: "A very important point in the philosophy of science is that progress consists of replacing an old theory by generalizing it, not by throwing it out."

Brock resolves the behavioral finance/efficient market theory split by suggesting that each occupies one end of the continuum. If we look at a market like foreign currency, then, yes, volatility is high and so is model uncertainty. People appear irrational. Markets seem unpredictable. At the other end of the spectrum, the market for Treasury bills is very stable and very predictable. Hence, the behavioral finance people appear to be right regarding the foreign currency market and EMTers appear correct in the short-term bond market. Brock is saying that a general theory can accommodate both claims.

Whenever we begin thinking that one way is right and the other wrong, we need to ask if there isn't a bigger picture that includes both.

How does this apply to investment selections?

Consider the airline industry. Once upon a time there was only one way to run an airline. The big players, United and American, knew the formula. They took advance seat reservations, they tailored the type of plane to the route, they sold through travel agents, they flew to big airports, and they provided meals and movies. Airline executives believed that this formula was the only formula that could work—and that is the first clue to make you suspect that thinking has become too rigid, too fundamental, too fixed. Sure enough, along comes Uncle Herb and starts Southwest. And what is Southwest's formula? Nearly the opposite. They give seats at check-in, they only fly 737s, they sell direct to the customer, they fly to small airports, and they don't provide meals and movies . . . just good old peanuts and soda!

Does the new formula work?

Over the past decade, American Airlines stock (AMR) has languished, trading at around $30 then and now. In the same time period, Southwest's stock (LUV) has gone from $2 to more than $20, a tenfold increase. Both/and thinking would suggest that some third possibility exists that would be even more powerful than either of these polarities.

Another realm in which both/and thinking has been extremely powerful is valuation tools for picking stocks. Combining the contrarian value models—low P/E and P/Book Value—with momentum indicators—Earnings Surprise and Price Momentum—has produced some outstanding tools that use the best elements of both. Jack Brush at Columbine was a pioneer in exploring this combination.

The point is that we must train ourselves to be on the watch for either/or thinking. When we spot it, an opportunity leaps out to find the peak of the triangle and discover a new solution that is more powerful than either point at the base. The new discovery requires a willingness and ability to hold the tension of the opposites until the new idea emerges. Our discussion of personality types suggests that lions are the least likely to wait for that new possibility. They want to decide and move on. The influence of the jesters (NP types) is critical in balancing the lions' need to close and take action.

The moral of this story? Creative investors are conscious in their decision making. Sometimes they must decide between two alternatives and move forward. Other times, though, they will see that the real gold is in identifying the opposing forces and then saying, "A third solution will emerge that is even more powerful than either of these two."

Then again, sometimes it's best to just crane your neck and see what the other guy is doing. That's the subject of Chapter 21.

EXERCISE

Go back to the list of beliefs that you wrote down in the last exercise of Chapter 18. Choose one that offers the potential of finding a worthy advocate on the other side. Schedule some time to meet with someone who holds that opposite view and debate your positions. Once you have done that and dug your heels in, then switch roles and argue the other side. Try to become objective about the arguments, seeing the validity of each. Now that you've clearly defined the duality (the either/or thinking), let go of both positions and brainstorm how the two might come together to give a bigger, more useful picture. Is there a new valuation technique or type of company that represents both/and thinking? Ask yourself questions like, "What if each of these positions has a valuable partial truth within it?" or "How can we combine these partial truths to develop a more powerful one?"

CHAPTER 22

"B" Is for Borrow from Other Disciplines

I not only use all the brains I have, but all I can borrow.
—Woodrow Wilson

Borrow from other disciplines. As simple as it sounds, it's amazing how few people do it. Instead, people—suffering from the "must-be-invented-here" syndrome—spend weeks, months, and years developing the same product or process that some other organization has already invented and marketed. Maybe it's a hangover from American's Puritan heritage, insisting that all progress must involve suffering. Maybe it's our pride: "I don't need any help. I can do this by myself." (All women with male drivers in the family can relate to this idea.) Perhaps it is because in grade school we learned that collaborating with your neighbor is rewarded with a trip to the principal's office.

Beats me.

In any event, all of us should make this our first stop when we are asked to innovate. We should ask, "Has anyone else done this anywhere?" or a related question, "Who is the best-in-class at this?"

The philosopher Nietzsche warned us not to read too many great books because it would deflate our self-esteem and kill our initiative. But the truth is that we can get wonderful inspirations from standing on the shoulders of the greats. Even the not-so-greats, who just happen to have some terrific ideas.

I cannot tell you how many times, when I've been asked to help teams brainstorm a new product or concept, this simple advice is overlooked. For example, I was helping a church develop a membership drive and I simply asked, "What are the techniques of the successful churches?" From the expressions on the participants' faces, you would have thought I had said, "By the way, everyone, Nietzsche was right: God *is* dead." No one had researched what other churches were doing. This question should always be the starting point. The great inventor Thomas Edison said, "Keep on the lookout for novel and interesting ideas that others have used successfully. Your idea has to be original only in its adaptation to the problem you're working on."

A famous example of this principle is the printing press. Johann Gutenberg combined two well-known inventions: the wine press and the coin stamp. His genius was simply in seeing how these two already existing devices could be combined to produce a third one. The world is full of these examples, like drive-through ATM machines borrowed from fast-food outlets.

The same will happen in the world of finance. Leslie Rahl, president of Capital Markets Risk Advisors, said in 1998, "I absolutely believe that we're going to take lessons in finance from other parts of science." Of course, it has happened many times already. Perhaps the most famous example is Professors Black and Scholes borrowing heat transfer equations from the world of physics to create the Black-Scholes Option Pricing Model.

If investors can shift into the open mode, described in Chapter 19, and ask themselves how new developments in other areas can be applied to the world of investing, they will be surprised. And delighted.

The applications may not be confined to new inventions, either. Consider the implications for research. Information is essential in investing, as Gordon Gekko eloquently reminded us in his "Greed is good" speech in the film *Wall Street*. Each time I hear of some clever process for gathering information, I ask, "How could this be applied elsewhere? In investing? In marketing? In my personal life?

As an example, IBM has made it possible for anyone to go on the Web and research existing technology patents. Why would IBM spend the money to do this? Altruism? Hardly. Big Blue tracks all the inquiries to monitor public curiosity. They want to know where they should be spending research dollars, and what better way than to let the public lead you? It reminds me of the architect who put sidewalks in between his buildings *after* the people had worn the grass bare, following the natural traffic patterns. Smart, huh? IBM apparently is doing the same thing on the electronic highway. How can the vast amount of information on the Web be used to determine buying interest in stocks, bonds, and other assets?

Investors are just beginning to tap the best practices of other disciplines. Seasoned investors (read: old farts) will need to stay open to the wisdom of the younger generation. The Ameritrade commercial mentioned earlier, which features funky young Stuart and his old, stodgy boss, is a perfect example of this synergy. Pay no attention to Shakespeare's advice about neither borrowing nor lending; instead, take to heart what Edison said about using ideas from other fields freely. In fact, this notion of creatively borrowing ideas from others ties neatly into the next tip: Ask for help.

EXERCISE

Try this exercise with your investment group. Brainstorm a list of current products or services that are new and successful. Examples:

- Blockbuster membership cards that are scannable and fit on your key ring.

- Pokémon trading cards.
- Palm Pilots.
- MP3 portable music players.

Then extract from your list what the benefit from each product is and what feature provides the benefit. Example: downloading music from the Internet. The benefit is convenience and customization. No longer do you have to go to the mall, park, walk, and stand in line to buy a CD with 2 songs that you like and 10 that stink. Now you can go to sites that design custom CDs with the songs you want. How does this feature relate to investment products and services? How does this feature relate to existing companies and industries? Will some firms become obsolete? (What does Encarta Online do to encyclopedia sales? Whoa!)

The key: Work with products and services that already exist and practice making associations.

CHAPTER 23

"A" Is for Ask for Help

Two men working as a team will produce more than three men working as individuals.

—Charles P. McCormick

Ask for help. Some of us, particularly of the male persuasion, shudder at the mere mention of this. (There is an old joke about why it takes so long for the sperm to fertilize an egg; the answer is because none of them will stop and ask for directions.) Investment professionals are trained, like good poker players, to keep their cards close to the vest. As Gordon Gekko said in the movie *Wall Street*, information is power. It's the competitive edge that we all crave.

A few times in my professional career I have been in possession of legitimate illegitimate information. One of these occasions was years ago, while I was meeting with a media analyst about Time Inc., back before it merged into Warner and then into AOL. (Younger portfolio managers note: Yes, this was *after* the Civil War.) I sat taking notes and the analyst droned on about the *Washington Post*, Times Mirror, and finally Time Inc. I remember the meeting as being especially unremarkable until this analyst said, "Now that Time Inc. has divested itself of Temple Inland, the forest products division . . . ." My ears pricked up like the family dog when it sees

195

the cat. My expression must have revealed my excitement because the next thing the analyst said was, "Oh crap! What day is it? Tuesday? Damn it! You can't tell anybody I said that. I forgot that they aren't announcing the divestiture until tomorrow." Usually Wall Street analysts are pretty unflappable, but this guy looked like he had a live cigarette down his pants, so I knew some serious beans had been spilled. It was the kind of information that would give Gordon Gekko moist palms. My point is simply that information is precious and must be protected at all costs. (As you could guess from looking at the car I drive, I didn't parlay that slip into a financial fortune.)

It's no surprise then that analysts tend to live their lives like expert gamblers, keeping poker faces and hiding their cards. The problem with this approach—a theme that this book drives home with a hammer—is that it lacks balance. In the same way that we need to be shrewd about when to use our different traits, like sensing versus intuition, we need to know when to be open and when to be focused. Likewise, we need to know when to keep our own counsel and when to share information and enlist help. At the risk of being blunt, I'll say that investment professionals wouldn't recognize the power of collaboration if it bit them in the behind.

This Lone Ranger approach ("I'll do it myself, without help") may be traced to the high value that investors place on being competent. Many investment professionals equate asking for help with being incompetent. Because they would rather endure third-degree burns than appear incompetent, they don't ask. Why do I believe this? A couple of examples should illustrate adequately. First is one from a playful chief financial officer (yes, they do exist) that I befriended years ago. He used to get bored during analyst interrogations, so he would mischievously drop in acronyms and lingo that were nonsense. His purpose? Just to see if anyone would stop him and ask, "What does that mean?" It tickled him to see these hot-shot analysts nodding and squinting their eyes, doing their best imitations of Wise King Solomon, while all the time he was talking gibberish. He said that in all his years, only a couple of analysts ever stopped him to ask "if the emperor had any clothes."

The technique that I use to get around the "emperor's clothes" phenomenon is something I call the Candid Camera technique. Remember Alan Funt on *Candid Camera*? A classic setup involved a person in a waiting room in which the pictures on the walls were moving slightly. Most of the participants noticed the movement and then, being human, buried their heads in their magazines. Ignore it. Pretend it isn't happening. It's always easier to do nothing, especially when you think that no one is watching.

When placed in a situation like this, we all like to think that we would do the courageous, mature thing. We would calmly point out to the office manager that something weird is going on with the pictures: namely, they seem to be shifting on the walls. Right. Sure. The truth is that we'd do what every other self-conscious person would do: get really interested in a magazine and hunker down.

Trying to look good and save face, aside from being an enormous energy drain, can be a huge impediment to creativity.

How do we overcome this all-too-human tendency? Remember our goal here: We're trying to find a way to avoid being buffaloed like the analysts in the story were by the mischievous CFO. What sort of mental technique could we employ to call his bluff?

My technique is to reframe the situation. I imagine that I am the subject (victim?) of a *Candid Camera* prank (or a prankster CFO). Everything changes when I ask myself, "If this were a setup, being filmed as a practical joke, how would I feel about it when I viewed it later? Would I feel foolish for not speaking up? Would I feel silly for not stating the obvious?" When I reframe it in this way, it helps me avoid the emperor's-clothes syndrome.

I had occasion to use this technique at a conference in which a speaker was presenting his outlook for Internet stocks. He placed a transparency on the overhead projector and began talking about the outlook for the company—according to the slide, eToys. A few minutes into his comments, I suspected that we were looking

at the wrong slide. A few minutes after that, I *knew* we were looking at the wrong one. As predicted, the audience hunkered down
and took notes harder. Although tempted to follow suit, I used the
Candid Camera reframing technique instead. I asked myself how
I would feel if this whole scene had been set up just to see I was
the perfect lemming. Wouldn't I feel stupid just going right over
the cliff, no questions asked? Of course. So I stuck a hand up and
pointed out the mistake. The speaker looked at his notes a few
times, squinted at the screen, replaced "eToys" with "eBay," thanked
me, and went on.

On this topic of asking for help, though, the real eye-popper
for me took place at a conference on creativity, hosted by the
American Productivity and Quality Center in Disney World. Rep-
resentatives from major companies like 3M, Microsoft, and Disney
were present. Meetings on various aspects of innovation were
conducted simultaneously. At the end of the day, there was a large
cocktail reception. The experience of attending that reception blew
my mind and certainly my belief system. Imagine a conservative
clergyman walking into a lurid orgy and you'll get a sense of my
shock. It was like two worlds colliding. I couldn't have been more
surprised if I had walked into the cantina scene in *Star Wars*. Why?
Their behavior was outrageous, inappropriate, crazy. How so? They
were all sharing information freely, as if they didn't understand
that information is the key to market success. They were showing
their cards to all the other poker players! They were shamelessly
playing "I'll show you mine if you'll show me yours," as if the
world were coming to an end. As an investment professional, I had
never seen this sort of exhibitionism before. I'm sure my mouth
was open wide enough for a basketball to be shoved in it. They
were posing questions to one another that had the emotional impact—to an investor—of asking, "What is your salary?" or "What
is your net worth?" To me, it seemed totally inappropriate, not to
mention highly dangerous, for them to be sharing best practices
with one another.

Viewed from a different perspective, they were asking for and receiving help on difficult issues in a truly collaborative way. Am I saying that investment professionals should run out and share all their hard-earned information? No. There is a place for cooperation and a place for competition. Choice is the issue. Knowing when to use each and having a choice is the key. My experience with investors is that they spend so much time in the competitive mode that they miss many opportunities to ask for help.

There is another arena in which investors could ask for help. As discussed in Chapter 5, investors could establish buddy systems to monitor their emotional reactions, the ones that could damage performance. (Watch out if a person's response to this topic is: "I don't have emotional reactions." We *all* have emotional reactions; it's just a matter of how we manage them.) Meir Statman, a professor of behavioral finance, suggests that investors recognize their capacity for (biased) emotional decision making and experiment with cooling-off periods, like the three-day time period the law provides for consumers to act on "buyer's regret." Statman writes, "The same argument applies to securities. People understand that cognitive errors and imperfect self-control interfere with good decisions" (*Behavioral Finance and Decision Theory in Investment Management*, AIMR Publications 1995). We could guard against these habits and avoid inferior decisions by buddying up with someone who knows us and our tendencies when emotional reactions are triggered. A case in point is the example from Chapter 5 about the portfolio manager who overreacted in the PharMor situation. He could have saved his firm hundreds of thousands of dollars by asking for help.

In what ways could you improve your level of creativity and investment results by collaborating with others? If top athletes and performing artists have coaches, doesn't it seem odd that top money managers don't? Again we could draw from the experience of John Cleese, the comedian, who now collaborates on all his creative projects. Two heads *are* better than one. Even if the other person is just a sounding board, she can play a crucially important role.

I believe that this principle of asking for help extends to the highest level. Call it prayer if you like, or simply a general request of the universe, but time after time, I have found that when I stop to put out a "formal" request for help, something magical occurs. Examples of this are given later in the book, but one that occurs to me now is a request that I made about money management and personality types. I wanted to find some fresh material that related money to personalities. I knew that somewhere, someone was thinking about these same issues—I just didn't know where or who. So one evening, sitting in my office, I made my intention known by saying it aloud: "I'd like some help with my research. I want information about money management and personality types, information that would tie in to the book I'm writing." (I get a kick out of our pets' reactions to my monologues. Our two cats and dog look around my home office with curious expressions that say, "Who the hell is he talking to?") Laugh if you will, but within an hour of making this "universal request" I received an email from the Myers-Briggs association in Florida informing me that Ken Doyle at the University of Minnesota had just published a book called *The Social Meanings of Money and Property*. The book not only examined people's relationship to money, based on four different temperaments (lions, foxes, owls, and dolphins), which was exactly my interest, but also viewed individuals and groups not as "static collections of traits but as dynamic systems of attributes-in-tension." Bingo.

Put simply, Doyle agrees with Csikszentmihalyi on the importance of complexity. Perhaps that's not put so simply, after all; let me try it again. *Complexity* is the ability to balance opposing forces, like the ability to be decisive and to be flexible. Complexity seems to explain the extraordinary ability of our master investors. Doyle's book addresses precisely this issue. Now, do you see why it was so weird that I would get this email within an hour of asking for help?

No.

No?

Okay, forget it. Pretend I never mentioned it. (Gee whiz, some people!)

EXERCISE

What resources do you have as an investor? What people are in your corner? List them.

- How could you enlarge this list?
- Could you learn some skill that would help? Better organization? Better time management? Personal coaching?
- Can you leverage the benefits of the people who are committed to your success?
- Is there a way to work with people who are considered your competitors? In what creative ways might you partner with them, so that you create a win-win scenario?

CHAPTER 24

"T" Is for Tools and Techniques

Determine that the thing can and shall be done, and then we shall find the way.

—Abraham Lincoln

"T" is for tools and techniques. Improving creativity, whether individually or in groups, requires processes. People with the best intentions may meet to brainstorm and get minimal results. Why? Because they don't have clear processes to guide them through the tough spots. One common mistake that's already been mentioned is allowing the idea generators and the idea evaluators to work simultaneously. The result is usually that any new idea, especially if it's radical, is dismissed immediately. Common reasons for dismissal are "It's too expensive," "It's been tried," and "It has *never* been tried." The outcome of these meetings is usually a headache, because two conflicting forces were undermining any progress. To see the problem clearly, remember the last time you were in a traffic jam that was caused by a broken streetlight. Instead of traffic flowing neatly through the intersection, guided by the green and red lights, drivers had to inch their way into the intersection, one by one, taking forever and giving new meaning to the words "road rage."

The same is true of ideas. If the process is clearly defined, then participants understand the sequence. First ideas will be generated, without criticism, and *then* they will be evaluated. The process flows rather smoothly.

The consulting firm that I mentioned earlier, Interaction Associates (IA), has been teaching organizations how to make meetings work for more than 20 years. In fact, the founders of IA, Michael Doyle and David Straus, literally wrote the book on it: *How to Make Meetings Work* (Dell 1976). IA's research has shown that 90 percent of the problems with meetings are process-related rather than content-related. The example that IA uses to make this point is cooking an egg. The egg is the content and the process could be one of many: boiling, scrambling, frying, and so on. To prove this point in the classroom, IA trainers will ask participants to name all the problems that make for bad meetings. Participants respond with a long list of items: no agenda, arriving late, losing focus, too long, sidebar discussions, no clear outcomes, no follow-through, and so forth. When the trainers then ask participants to state whether these problems involve processes or content, invariably the response is "process." In other words, meeting participants usually agree on *what* to discuss (content), but they differ on *how* to discuss it. Hence, meetings go awry and live down to the reputation chronicled in *Dilbert* cartoons: horribly inefficient wastes of time. It's a small wonder that Warren Buffett says the best meeting he attends each week is the one with himself in his mirror.

Tools (processes) are important enablers of creativity. This may sound painfully obvious to readers, but my experience with investors is that they are very unsophisticated with regard to meeting technology. In fact, many investment meetings are the equivalent of eating with your fingers and tossing the bones on the floor. I've been in investment meetings where the attendees weren't even introduced to one another; there was no agenda; no use of visuals to help create common understanding; no clear roles (such as who is facilitating the meeting); long, boring downloads of information;

and on and on. It's no wonder that little is accomplished and that meetings have a bad reputation.

Another rarity among investment professionals is planning for meetings. A rule of thumb for any meeting is an hour of planning for every hour of meeting time. Sound outrageous? Well, if you consider the expense of gathering 10 people in a room for 2 hours, it doesn't seem unreasonable to have the meeting host take an hour to plan for it. After all, you wouldn't invite 10 people over for dinner and then greet them at the door with, "Hey, glad you could make it, let's look through the fridge and see what we've got." This isn't really a professional facilitator's rant, either; a lot of it is just common sense.

Okay, we now know that we need tools. What are some useful tools? We've discussed a number of them so far in this book. The filters, for example, are a good tool (see Chapter 10). Using Myers-Briggs preferences, you can design a process whereby meeting members agree to work with one filter at a time, thereby avoiding a mental traffic jam. The first filter, sensing, could be used to discuss the facts. No new ideas or evaluations, just the map of reality . . . what "is." Then participants could agree to brainstorm and play with new ideas; this is the realm of intuition. You might even consider a separate meeting with the people who like brainstorming and are naturally inclined toward it. Finally, you could evaluate and refine ideas and test them in a practical sense. Thinking types are excellent in this role.

Surrounding this whole process is the question of how much time should be spent playing with ideas and how much in moving on with the task at hand. Perceivers like to try on new ideas and are comfortable with experimenting. Judgers prefer to close and get on with the implementation. A facilitator can help balance these energies in the project. Both energies have their place and are useful.

What about brainstorming itself? Are there more effective ways to come up with fresh ideas?

A good general technique for starting any project is a *brain dump*. Here is the process. Collect the team members in a room and equip them with markers and pads of 3-by-5-inch sticky notes. One wall of the room should be covered with flipchart paper, unless the wall is naturally friendly to stickies. Spend a few minutes on introductions, if the team is new, and set the context for the brainstorming activity. Decide on the topic to be brainstormed. The wording makes a difference, of course. Each of the following might be related to increasing the stock price of your company, but they would be very different discussions:

- How can the company increase sales?
- How can the company reduce expenses?
- How can the company grow faster?
- How can the company earn a higher price/earnings multiple?

When groups are first beginning a project, I suggest starting with as wide a topic as possible, because the process itself will define and structure future, more focused discussions. Start big and map out the entire territory. In fact, this idea came to me after watching a company called Learning Maps make a presentation at Disney World. Learning Maps is in the business of creating visual representations of a company's position in the marketplace. They meet with company executives and work with them, in a creative fashion, to gain agreement about the nature of their business and how it would look as a board game. What is their goal? Who are the competitors? What industry conditions are changing? How does regulation affect them? What are the future threats? What are the key levers that determine sales growth?

Developing and producing Learning Maps for a company is often time-consuming and expensive, but companies seem happy with the results because management and employees have—perhaps for the first time—a common vision. To understand the power of a common vision, imagine playing chess without a chessboard. How difficult would it be to remember all the moves in your head? You move a pawn. Your opponent moves a pawn. You move your knight. Your opponent moves her bishop. Already it would be getting difficult to remember the board and plan the next move. How about 10 moves from now? Nearly impossible, right? There is a reason why the generals in those old war movies moved the plastic pieces around on the big map. They wanted everyone to be looking at the same view of reality. The map provides a rich tool for clarifications, discussions, disagreements, and strategies.

The point here is that with a brain dump, teams can create a unified vision of their project in less than an hour. This process compares favorably with the countless hours taken up in traditional meetings, where a group sits around a conference table and talks endlessly.

Also, the brain-dump process is simple. Propose a topic, check to make sure that participants understand and agree that it's the "right" one, then turn the group loose for 10 minutes with their markers and stickies. Encourage them to put at least 10 ideas on the wall (one per minute). Ideally, each idea should have a noun and a verb. Example: If you are brainstorming a topic like company morale, don't write a one-word note like "happy." (Yes, it would be nice if everyone were happy, but the idea by itself doesn't really give direction.) Better to write, "Shorten the work week" or "Balance family and work." Also, instruct participants to write one or two ideas that are ridiculous. These ideas are great to loosen up the group and get them laughing. (Remember Harrison Owen's advice: If it's not fun, it's not working!) And sometimes it's the goofy ideas that lead to the breakthroughs.

Here's a brief digression on the importance of goofy ideas. A colleague at Interaction Associates tells of a brainstorming session in which the group was trying to raise money for a charity. All the usual fundraising ideas had been rounded up and then, as a joke, a man called out, "Rob a bank." The group laughed. Silly idea.

But then another participant remembered that his brother-in-law worked for a bank that was looking for a charitable cause to support. Eventually, this goofy idea led to the bank sponsoring the charity. (Remember the discussion of the inner critic in Chapter 15? How easy it would have been for this man to squash his own idea and not say, "Rob a bank." Fortunately for the group, he took a chance and hollered it out.)

When the group has "dumped" its ideas on the wall, take a moment to clarify them. Ask the group if there are any ideas that need explanation. Also, check for duplicates. If two ideas are identical, there is no need to have them both on the wall. Checking for duplicates and clarifying shouldn't take more than 10 minutes.

Sometimes the process derails here because the clarifying turns into advocating. Participants explain not only what their idea is but also why it is such a good one. The facilitator needs to jump in quickly and remind participants that there will be an opportunity later to advocate and prioritize the ideas. Right now, the task is to understand them. In our earlier Myers-Briggs language, this phase emphasizes sensing (the blue filter). Just the facts, ma'am—no interpretations.

The next portion of the brain dump is to make some sense out of the ideas that have been thrown on the wall. Before suggesting a process for that, let me just explain the rationale for this first phase of silently filling out the notes and posting them. First, it invites the introverts to participate. Remember, introverts tend to prefer writing and internal dialogue to talking and processing out loud. Also, silence tends to help us move into the right hemisphere, where creativity lives. When we focus and talk, we move into the left hemisphere, where logic and verbal skills hang out. Finally, having the participants watch as the ideas go up on the wall allows them to build on one another's thoughts, so synergy can take place.

The notes on the wall are the key factors that the group has identified for the project, vision, strategy, or whatever they are brainstorming. The question now is, "How do these key factors relate to one another?" How does the group make sense of them? At this point I ask the group to shout out two ideas, from the stickies on the wall, that seem related. Example: The topic for the exercise is valuation of Internet stocks, and two ideas that were posted are "Price to Sales Ratio" and "Price to Earnings Ratio." I would place these notes, which seem to be related, one above the other, in their own column. It's best to stick them to the wall surface separately, rather than to each other. If too many notes are stuck onto each other, the entire column eventually falls off the wall. (Aren't you thrilled to get this caliber of professional advice without consultant fees?)

To add creativity to this process, I tell the group that the columns they are now forming can have only four notes in each. This forces the group to make fine distinctions rather than lumping all the ideas under two big headings, like "Internet Stocks with Foreign Operations" and "Internet Stocks with Domestic Operations Only." These sorts of general headings may be accurate, but they're not particularly useful. An important point (which harks back to our earlier discussion of top-down versus bottom-up investors from Chapter 10) is this: Participants invariably try to name the general categories before they have really done the pairings of ideas. Someone will look at the mass of notes and start dictating categories: We need one for "P/E ratios," one for "Price to Sales ratios," and so on. I suggest that you enforce the instruction of simply pairing up related ideas. In other words, stay at the level of details and don't jump to the intuitive level of concepts. That comes next.

Some participants will get into this pairing and organizing exercise (the S and J types love it) and others will step back and get a coffee refill. That's fine. That's the power of self-organizing teams. It's neat to watch. Without any explicit leadership or micromanagement, this task of organizing the data occurs quickly and effectively. The right people step up and get it done. It's like watching Adam Smith's invisible hand at work. The facilitator shouldn't interfere too much. If someone wants to move notes that have already been placed, that's fine. Others have the option of moving them back again!

When the sorting and organizing are finished, pass out some stickies that are a different color from the originals and preferably larger (4-by-6-inchers work well). Ask the participants to pair up in threes (as Yogi Berra used to say) and ask these small groups to name columns that they want to work with. Here is the part of the exercise that intuitives will like. It involves finding a pattern. Have them look at the ideas in their assigned column and identify the relationship between them. For example, our sample column with "Price to Earnings Ratio" and "Price to Sales Ratios" might be labeled "Traditional Valuation Methods" to reflect the relationship of the ideas in it. These titles are called *headers*. Once created, I move the headers to a separate portion of the wall and give the participants a moment to look at them. Again, if there is a need for clarification, it takes place at this point.

The final phase of a brain dump is to ask the participants to consider the relationship among the headers. In this way, the group is beginning to create its own learning map. The group members are looking at their collective "reality"—the key factors involved in the topic—and discussing what the map should look like. I give them stickies with arrows drawn on them and ask the group once again to go to the wall and arrange the headers in some logical order. It could be chronological, cause and effect, prioritized . . . whatever is appropriate. This exercise is not done in silence. It is important to discuss and reach agreements in this phase, so talking is encouraged. Usually this final phase takes about 15 minutes to complete. Therefore, the total time for the brain dump is less than an hour.

The brain dump is an exercise in "visible thinking." Although it's simple, it invariably results in powerful insights for groups. I believe that's because common understanding and agreement are such powerful motivating factors for groups. The brain dump often is a powerful starting point for rich discussions about strategy and change. It often points out clear "next steps" that the group needs to take.

Sometimes the brain dump provides the solution and nothing more is needed. I facilitated such a session with a group of training professionals at a Fortune 500 company. Each of the five people thought that they were in for a long afternoon of political intrigue, negotiating, bargaining, and positioning. Their task was to design and agree on a core curriculum for training the employees and leaders of the company. In their minds, I would be facilitating a meeting with debates, conflict, and possibly even breakdowns.

The result was quite the opposite. I suggested the brain dump exercise as a way to start. I called the exercise "creating an 'is' map"—that is, a map showing us what the territory looks like right now, what "is." We went through the process that I just described. About an hour later, when all the ideas had been sorted into headers and then organized, a solution popped out. The headers had been arranged chronologically, with a clear map of how to proceed. First, additional research with employees and leaders must be conducted, then courses have to be designed to deliver the desired outcomes, measurement systems have to be in place to monitor the progress and success, and a feedback loop has to be established so that employees and leaders can participate in continuous improvement. This solution may seem unremarkable or fairly obvious to the reader, but it came as a tremendous relief to the five professionals involved. They didn't end up in a war with one another. They didn't even end up in a skirmish. Instead, they were motivated to divide up the work and focus their energy on the real task ahead: marketing this proposal to the senior leaders. Which, I might add, they did successfully. Here is a letter I received, commenting on the process:

> I wanted to take a moment and express my appreciation for all of the support you have provided to the Education Design and

Delivery area this year. Specifically, the work this summer regarding our Employee Development initiative.

In July, we requested that you facilitate a meeting regarding the challenge of building a corporate wide Employee Development Process. You had a lively crew to work with including several Directors and Senior Managers that would be very opinionated.

We loved the "Visible Thinking" facilitation method you took us through and felt your approach was perfect for our needs.

As a results of your efforts we were able to

1. Develop a shared vision - no small task!
2. Prioritize 15 components of work
3. Create a visual model of our strategy
4. Establish an implementation timeline

In summary, the "Visible Thinking" process allowed us to successfully navigate through a crucial building phase of this initiative with relative ease.

The point, again, in all of this is that creativity depends on creating a safe place where basic tools can be used for generating and processing ideas. The brain dump, with its emphasis on creating a map by making our thoughts visible, is a powerful and efficient tool to keep in your brainstorming kit.

This chapter has covered a few tools and techniques for group creativity. The next chapter gets personal with a few techniques that I've found useful.

CHAPTER **25**

Getting Personal

I will tell you what I have learned myself. For me, a long five- or six-mile walk helps. And one must go alone and every day.
—Brenda Ueland, *Tips on the Creative Life* (Graywolf 1938)

Perhaps the most important rule about the creative process is that it will differ for each person. The premise of this book is that diversity is real: Different personality styles demonstrate different communication, conflict, and creative patterns. And the differences matter, both for individual efforts and for group effectiveness.

This premise is highlighted when I have workshop participants draw their creative processes. This simple exercise (see the exercise at the end of this chapter) is the most powerful way I know of to show the group that everyone's process is unique. One person draws a tornado, indicating that when she is in the midst of creating, it is like a whirlwind, with all kinds of ideas flying, chaotic, energetic, and exciting. Another draws an oil well, indicating that some efforts were like dry holes with nothing coming out of them, whereas other efforts hit rich geysers of oil. Other visual metaphors include pieces of a puzzle that have to be interlocked and file drawers with all kinds of odd information stored away, waiting to be used.

When I first did the exercise, I surprised myself and drew a spider on a web. I hate spiders, and yet the image of storing information bits on a web and then retrieving them seemed to fit. (Interesting that, years later, the "Web" would become the name for the network that allows us to trade information electronically all over the world.) We all approach creativity in a slightly different fashion, and therefore we need to do a bit of introspection to see how best to support our own process. What specific techniques do you use to boost your creativity? How do you come up with investment ideas? How do you file them so that they can be useful later? Here are some of my most important techniques and tools.

First, and most powerful by far, is my hand-held recorder. Don't walk, run to your nearest electronics store and get a portable device for recording your ideas. It doesn't have to be the expensive, elaborate one that also performs strategic planning, project management, and valuation of technology stocks. The cheap one will do fine. Why do you need a recorder? Why not just a pen and paper? Simple: Pen and paper don't work while you're driving. They don't work well while you are walking down the street. They especially don't work well in the middle of the night. You need a device that will capture ideas when they strike at 3 A.M. and the room is pitch black.

Don't for a minute fall into the trap of assuming that you will remember in the morning, or when you park the car and get into the restaurant. You won't. Worse yet, you won't even remember that you didn't remember. The idea will simply be gone. Sir Francis Bacon (English philosopher and statesman, 1561–1626) observed: "A man would do well to carry a pencil in his pocket and write down his thoughts of the moment."

In fact, the only reason I am able to include this quotation here is because I grabbed my recorder and captured it during a lecture. So, carry a small recording device at all times. Or at least a pencil.

Here is the not-so-obvious reason why you need a recorder. If you're like me (and I know I am), you often find yourself in the following scenario, or a very similar one: You're ordering a Mrs. Fields cookie at the mall when suddenly you get a great idea. You don't have a pen or a recorder with you, so you fixate on the idea, repeating it to yourself, trying not to lose it. You become a zombie, walking through the mall staring into space and mumbling to yourself. If you have a cell phone, you can call your own phone number and leave the idea as a message. Not a bad option as an emergency measure, but not good as a regular routine. It takes too long, and there is always the chance that someone will pick up the phone or pick up the message. What's the lesson? When your brain is fixed on one idea, it's not open and receptive to other good ideas. If you're really like me, this is a little embarrassing. You jam up your brain for the entire shopping trip, then halfway home from the mall, some jerk cuts you off in traffic, which provokes you to invoke sacred personages at top volume, overloading the RAM memory in your brain and forcing the really good idea out your left ear. The upshot? You arrive home with no recollection that you ever had a really good idea. (There's a story of the time when Gurdjieff, the Russian philosopher, was practicing his powers of concentration. He assigned himself the task of focusing only on his breathing as he walked in the city. A few minutes into his walk, he noticed a new tobacco shop and stopped in to see the selection. Two days later he remembered that he had been doing a concentration exercise!)

The all-important point here is that ideas are like Kodak moments—they only come once in a lifetime. You must capture them or they are gone. So carry a recorder with you at all times and sleep with one beside your bed. Okay, enough said.

The next basic tool is a four-color pen. Cost: about $1.99. Buy them at any drugstore or office supply store. I give them out to participants in my creativity workshops. Why a four-color pen? Because it's hard to find 10-color pens! If they were readily available I would recommend 10 colors. Seriously though, do you remember those yellow-and-green boxes of Crayola crayons you had as a kid? With 64 colors and a sharpener in the back? The black crayon always wore down first, so you'd be peeling the paper and sharpening it while the gold and peach colors were still fresh. If you need any proof that our society crushes out creativity, just look at the average executive's pen: a gold Cross ballpoint with black ink. One color. From 64 down to 1. Bo-o-o-ring!

This pen is for more than just the fun of different colors. There's a reason why advertisers pay for four-color artwork and why presentations use multicolored pie charts. Color enhances the effectiveness of the message. Color helps the mind to organize information. Sports teams wear different-colored jerseys so that the players (and referees) can quickly tell friend from foe. All streetlights and stop signs use red to make their messages obvious and to convey that message quickly. Phone books are printed on white and yellow paper so that we can tell from 10 feet away if it's the residential or business listings. Yellow highlighters show us the key passages in articles. If you want a boost to your creativity, use the four-color pen as part of your process. I am never without mine, and I've noticed that many of my course graduates now carry their four-color pens at all times.

How do I use this marvelous tool? First, the colors in the pen, with one exception, correspond perfectly to the filters discussed in Chapter 10. Remember the blue, red, and green filters, representing the investigator, the activator, and the evaluator? If you toss in the black ink as the creator (ordinarily yellow), then you've got a system for recording ideas based on the filter system. Write the facts in blue ink, new ideas in black, critical comments in green, and action steps in red.

Consider also the discussion of the inner critic in Chapter 15. My suggestion was to use the Voice Dialogue technique to befriend your critic and turn it into your inner ally, your inner mentor and discipline coach. I use the journaling technique that the Stones describe. (Another popular approach was developed by Ira Progroff, a disciple of Carl Jung's.) I chose the following colors to represent each "part" of my psyche. The Aware Ego part of me, the part that just observes and doesn't get involved, is blue. Blue is a neutral color from the filter that just looks at facts. I chose the black ink to represent the critic. Black is a serious, heavy color for me (and for lots of other people), so I switch to the black ink when I am writing the thoughts of the critic. I use green to represent the gentler, tender side of myself—the innocent side, the playful child. Green is a color I associate with spring and flowers and new life, so this fits for me. Sometimes when journaling I will check in with this playful side of myself just to give it some attention and see if it needs anything. It's hard to be creative if you are starving this part of yourself. One writer/consultant I know calls this part of himself "the kid in the basement." He will figuratively "toss" projects down the stairs to this creative kid to see what he comes up with. Often he is astonished by the freshness of the "kid's" ideas.

If all this sounds weird to you, then I suggest there's a whole side to your creativity that you haven't explored. (I learned all this stuff on board the Mother Ship after I was abducted . . .) Watterson, author of the Calvin and Hobbes comic strip, attributes his success to this inner dialogue process. He wrote in the preface to his last book that he let his characters "write their own material. I put them in situations and listen to them." Calvin's answers were things that Watterson, the adult, would never have thought of. In any event, I use the green to capture the responses from my own inner Calvin.

The color red I reserve for dreams. Many sages from many different traditions have said that dreams are messages directly from the Creator. The literature about creative geniuses is rife with examples of breakthroughs that resulted from dreams. An example is Kekulé, who proposed the ring structure of the benzene molecule after he saw a snake grabbing its own tail in a dream. Edison's acknowledgment of the importance of dreams was mentioned earlier; he used the rocks-and-pans procedure for waking himself from the dream state so that he could capture those insights.

My own experience with dreams has been noteworthy and

instructive. Often my dreams have given clear and sound advice about practical matters. Years ago, when I was in crisis, I found myself in the office of a psychotherapist. I saw him three times and had clear misgivings about him. I didn't trust him. Of course, when I voiced this concern, I got the standard Catch-22 response: "You have trust issues and you will have to work through them with me." This left me in a very uncomfortable position. The "expert" was telling me that I needed his help, but I didn't trust the expert. After my third visit, I went to bed wrestling with this issue and had a dream in which I was instructed to check the Biblical passage, Job 12:17. Curious, I looked it up and found these words: "He makes fools of counselors and judges."

I interpreted this message as a clear signal to end the relationship. My unconscious was telling me that this counselor was a fool. I stopped seeing him. The result? Several months later I learned that a professional review committee had censored this therapist for molesting female patients.

That's why I use red ink to record dreams. I suppose this practice is a bit like publishers using red ink to highlight the words of Jesus in the New Testament. Dreams represent wisdom from a higher, vaster source—maybe divine, maybe the Jungian "universal mind" that Lear spoke of.

Still another use of the four-color pen is for mindmapping. I do all my brainstorming on 14-by-11-inch sketch pads. I place the project name in the center—a workshop, speech, article, business plan, industry review, whatever—and then begin to dump my ideas on the page, however they occur to me. Sometimes the pattern is chronological, as with a workshop outline, but sometimes it is random, as in an industry review. I use colors to help organize the information. If I am co-leading a workshop, I can use two colors to represent the material that I might present versus the material presented by my partner. Red often indicates audience participation, some activity that the group will do. With this technique, I can see, just by the colors on the page, whether I have a good balance

of both trainers presenting, plus activities to involve the participants. Also, when space gets tight on the page, it is easy to squeeze
in more information if the new information is a different color from
the lettering that surrounds it.

Frankly, I am amazed that more people don't use a four-color
pen. Why? Because people, sooner or later, migrate toward what
works. Flip charts, sticky notes, emails, Websites, and the like all
exist because people value them. They use them and get results.
Given the value that I've received from the use of four colors, I
don't understand why they aren't more popular. Could it be simple
vanity? Let's face it, they don't look too great. Schlocky, fat, plastic
pens. No fashion statement, to be sure. But they work.

Another tip for personal creativity is to find ways to interrupt
your patterns. I know, this is so painfully obvious as to be insulting. You're right. I take it back. Do the same old thing forever,
see if I care. Actually, I read articles all the time that make this
point (it's probably THE main point to be made about creativity),
but they give the stupidest examples. Here's an article on un-
locking your creativity from a Florida paper: "Change your patterns . . . . Take a new route to work: better yet, bike to work or
take the bus instead. Go to the park, take your shoes off and eat
your lunch instead of huddling over your desk."

Oh, brother. My first reaction to this article was to call the
writer and ask him to rewrite it with his shoes off. Better yet, take
his tie off, because I don't think enough oxygen is reaching his
brain. I mean, really, has he ever been to Chicago in January? You
want to try biking in January? You want to try lunch in the park
with your shoes off? With three feet of snow and the wind chill at
30 below? Go right ahead, Admiral Byrd. While you're at it, find
a new route, preferably one with unplowed roads and snowdrifts
over your head. Also, I wonder if this author has ever in his life
taken his own advice and purposely tried a new route to work. If
so, did it do any good?

How did this uninspiring author ever come up with the idea

that taking off your shoes in the park is going to stimulate break-through thinking? How can somebody writing an article about creativity be so uncreative? My point, and I do have one, is that platitudes like "Change your patterns" must be supported with real-world examples to be of any use. Otherwise they just waste our time. I don't want platitudes, I want to know what this author has actually done in real life that helped him get new ideas. That would be a juicy meal. Instead, he offers up these rice cakes. I had the same complaint about the advice to "turn off" my inner critic. Tell me how!

So, what do I do to break patterns? First off, I admit that I hate breaking patterns. I like my routines. So did my father. When I ragged on him about the rut he'd been living in for 20 years of retirement, he responded, "Buzz off, I like my rut." Routines are comfortable. William James advised that we use *lots* of routine in our lives so that we would have energy for the "important" stuff. But creativity *is* part of the important stuff, and messing with routines means using different thinking. Changing habits feels awkward at best and painful at worst. If you don't believe that, go have a baby or get a puppy or use your opposite hand for a day. Your routines will be smashed like an egg off a 40-foot building and you'll be pissed off. You'll be forced to let go of the comfy patterns and wrestle with life on an hour-to-hour basis. You'll have to wake up.

When I was writing and recording music albums, I found that I could break my patterns by composing on different instruments. If I wrote only on the guitar, the chord progressions and melodies would revolve around familiar finger placements. My hands would automatically grab a D-major or E-major chord almost by them-selves. The same was true of piano: Certain chord progressions—different from those of guitar—were patterns. What I did then, to come up with new melodies, was alternate between the two instruments. It was much like alternating between two preferences, say sensing (details) and intuiting (big-picture). By forcing my-self out of the groove, to another instrument, I got fresh and energetic sounds. Stretching that example even further, sometimes I would start with percussion and write a melody to sing along with a groove that I had created on a drum machine. The point is that I had to manipulate my own patterns or I'd end up with variations on the same old theme, rather than fresh, new songs.

In investing, I used similar tricks. For starters, I changed indus-tries frequently. I went from publishing to retail to insurance and banking to forest products and so on. Each time it was a pain to start all over, because I had learned so much about the preceding industry. I knew the basic facts about the companies, had met their officers, had drawn up spreadsheets, and had written reports. It was easy to sit back and be the expert. Problem was, I always got stale. I couldn't avoid falling into the same patterns, so I had to move on to territory where nothing was familiar and therefore nothing was habitual. Some people may be very creative with the same industry over time. I wasn't. And this is part of my point: Each of our styles is different. You have to be introspective enough to examine what works and what is simply the result of being lazy or afraid.

Here is another tip on enhancing personal creativity. Develop an openness to a power greater than yourself that can provide help. This is what Lee Hill, president of Lee Hill ad agency, tells his employees when their idea wells run dry: "When you want a great idea, pray."

The idea that all creativity ultimately comes from a "Creator" is what I turn to in the last part of this book. Much of what I've written so far is solid, standard stuff that you'd read in any book on creativity. These last chapters strive to take a leap and explore some new territory, an equal partnership between the left and right brain, between logic and intuition.

THE CREATIVE INVESTMENT TEAM

EXERCISE: WHAT KIND OF INVESTOR ARE YOU?

This is a good exercise to do with your investment team. It's intended to make you spend a few minutes reflecting on each person's different approach to investing. (I don't mean low P/E versus high P/E. I mean what's underneath that—what is your thought process?)

Take a moment to consider your investment approach.

- How do you come up with new ideas?
- What was your last creative idea?
- How do you gather information?
- What are the steps in your creative process?

Now, stretch your thinking a bit. Answer these questions:

- As an investor, what kind of animal are you?
- What kind of car would you be?
- What competitive sport is most like investing?

Finally, draw a picture of your investment process. What images, metaphors, and diagrams would help us understand your approach? More importantly, which ones help *you* understand your own inner workings?

This exercise is useful in two ways. First, it gives you insight into your own creative thought process. (One client, after doing this exercise, realized that her best ideas came during walks, so she made walking a regular part of her brainstorming.) Second, as you listen to your colleagues, you'll realize the rich diversity in creative styles of thinking. Most groups of fewer than 10 people have very different responses to the preceding questions. The work environment should support the thinking styles of the team members.

The Intuitive Investor:
Whole-Brained Investing

CHAPTER 26

Quantum Investing

The most beautiful thing we can experience is the mysterious.
—Albert Einstein

My first musings on creativity, spirituality, and investing began years ago when, following Edison's advice to look for ideas in other disciplines, I discovered the similarities between investing and physics. At Thanksgiving, I visit my cousins, two of whom are physicists. (The third cousin—the dumb one—programs mainframe computers.) When I was an active money manager, they used to ask me about my portfolio's performance in the same sympathetic voice Tom Cruise might have used to ask "Rain Man" about his pet mouse. One year, though, was worse than usual because my older physicist cousin had recently been quoted in *Business Week*. This meant, coincidentally, that at about the time he was being interviewed by a leading magazine in my field of endeavor, I was opening a deadbeat letter from that magazine's collection department.

This same older cousin wrote his doctoral thesis on some mysterious missing elementary particle that exists theoretically but has never actually been observed (sort of like excess returns in paper portfolios). When I first learned of his topic, several Thanksgivings ago, I remember offering to help look for the missing particle. I was only kidding, of course. But the offer was met by the icy stare of a *serious-minded* physicist, the kind whose pocket protector says, "Nobel Prize or Bust." As remedial action, my cousin recommended several books on physics, including *The Tao of Physics* and *The Dancing Wu Li Masters: An Overview of the New Physics*.

What struck me as I read these books on the evolution of physics were the similarities between physics and investing. Consider, for example, the model for investing prior to Harry Markowitz's Nobel prize-winning work on efficient frontiers. Portfolio managers used to construct their portfolios on a stock-by-stock basis, without considering the effect of stocks' interaction with each other. The importance of the covariance between stocks and the resulting benefits of diversification was often ignored, as Gerald Loeb's dictum from the 1950s indicates: "Diversification is undesirable. One or two, or at most three or four, securities should be bought" (quoted in Ellis, *Classics*, Dow Jones Irwin 1989).

With the advent of Modem Portfolio Theory (MPT), stocks are no longer considered separate and distinct, but rather are evaluated on the basis of how their interaction with other stocks in the portfolio affects such variables as tracking error, beta, and alpha. (In the 1950s, when my father managed money professionally, the terms *alpha* and *beta* brought to his mind fond memories of Greek fraternities, and "pairs analysis" was the favorite activity when sorority women arrived at a party. To his last day, my father believed that "efficient frontier" had something to do with the Louisiana Purchase.)

Consider the parallels with the evolution of classical Newtonian physics into modern quantum physics. Classical physics saw the scientist as standing apart from the physical world, carefully measuring its phenomena. It was thought that events were separate and distinct and could be accurately quantified. The model for the universe was that of a giant machine whose movements could be studied and known with certainty. This view changed as Einstein's relativity theory and Heisenberg's Uncertainty Principle became accepted. Modern physics, like Modern Portfolio Theory, recognizes that interaction is critical to the understanding of physical reality. "Material objects are not distinct entities, but are inseparably linked to their environment; . . . [T]heir properties [must] be understood in terms of this interaction with the rest of the world," writes Fritz Capra in *The Tao of Physics* (Bantam 1975).

Risk and return offer another parallel between investing and physics. Until Sharpe formalized the relation between risk and return in the Capital Asset Pricing Model (CAPM), relatively little attention was paid to these Siamese twins of investing. Consider this dictum from T. Rowe Price, a legend in growth-stock investing: "We believe that it [growth-stock investing] is the soundest and safest plan for the average investor." Price suggested that stocks with the longest duration (i.e., low dividends, high growth) and highest betas were the safest investments, which is clearly not the accepted view today. In defense of T. Rowe Price, at least he *included* risk in his investment philosophy; many of the investment practitioners in the 1950s and before ignored the subject altogether, overlooking the profound truth, as stated by Charlie Ellis, that "in the investment game, risk and return are inseparable" (*Classics*, 1989).

In physics, the relation between time and space was largely ignored or, at best, misunderstood. Then Einstein's theories showed that "space and time are treated on an equal footing and connected inseparably. In relativistic physics, we can never talk about space without talking about time and vice-versa" (Capra, *The Tao of Physics*).

Another similarity between the two disciplines is the distinction between "micro" and "macro" truths. At the macro level, Newton's laws of classical physics, which reduce all phenomena to the motions and interactions of hard, indestructible atoms, successfully explained the world as we knew it—that is, events such as falling apples. Classical physics began to crumble only when scientists started exploring the micro world inside the atom. In part, it was technological progress, in the form of more sophisticated equipment, that allowed scientists to discover the shortcomings of Newton's laws when applied to this micro world.

Similarly, "classical" investors, in the days before computers could crunch through reams of data and provide mind-numbingly detailed analyses, believed that earnings (when properly defined) explained stock price movements. T. Rowe Price stated that "the earnings factor, in the long run, determines the investment value of a share in a business" (quoted in Ellis, *Classics*). Of course, he's largely right. At the macro level—which in this analogy means a longer time frame—earnings do drive stock prices; as shown in a working paper by Easton, Harris, and Ohlson (Nov. 1989), the variance in earnings explains 63 percent of the variance in stock price movements. However, the same study shows that, at the micro level (i.e., less than one year), earnings explain less than 3 percent of the movement in stock prices. Thus, in both investing and physics, different forces seem to be operating at the macro and micro levels.

These differences have led practitioners in both disciplines to ever-greater efforts to unite their findings into one "unified" theory. This grand theory would presumably explain all behavior on all levels. As I was pondering these issues, during cocktails at a quantitative methods conference, one of the presenters was agonizing over this very point, lamenting that he might have to go back to school to get still more education in quantitative methods so that he could "crack the code" in investing. Underlying his angst was the clear belief that the stock market was orderly and law-abiding.

At this point in the conversation, I mentioned some of the similarities between physics and investing (the ones I just described) and suggested that possibly there is no single solution to the investment riddle. A latecomer to the discussion interjected that this issue was, in fact, the critical distinction between physics and investing: Because physics is a natural science, there are answers (though scientists may never uncover them). In contrast, investing is not an exact science, and therefore it does not have "final" answers. Investing is an art, not a science, as the saying goes. At that moment, Phil Fortuna, director of quantitative research at Scudder, Stevens & Clark and a former physics major, chimed in with a lucid explanation of the Heisenberg Uncertainty Principle. (This was very lucky for me, as I was dangerously close to trying to explain it myself.) This principle states that when

> observing a subatomic particle, one may choose to measure—among other quantities—the particle's position and its momentum (a quantity defined as the particle's mass times its velocity). [But] these two quantities can never be measured simultaneously with precision. We can either obtain a precise knowledge about the particle's position and remain completely ignorant about the particle's momentum (and thus about its velocity), or vice versa; or we can have a rough and imprecise knowledge about both quantities. The important point now is that this limitation has nothing to do with the imperfection of our measuring techniques. It is a principle limitation which is inherent in the atomic reality [Capra, *The Tao of Physics*].

The last two sentences seem to address exactly the anguished quantifier's concern about his shortcomings in math. As in physics, the reality of investing may be that there is no Golden Rule that applies to all situations, no matter how clever we are.

Another problem in both disciplines is the difficulty of measuring effect—in other words, isolating what causes what. In the relativistic world of modern physics and investing, things get a bit amorphous. Consider this description of the behavior of the electron by physicist Robert Oppenheimer:

> If we ask, for instance, whether the position of the electron remains the same, we must say "no"; if we ask whether the electron's position changes with time, we must say "no"; if we ask whether the electron is at rest, we must say "no"; if we ask whether it is in motion, we must say "no" [Oppenheimer, *Science and the Common Understanding*, Simon & Schuster 1954].

This paradox is a little like saying that a certain person is not tall, nor of average height, nor short. This is clearly unsettling; it even unnerved Einstein. Nevertheless, modem physics accepts the Uncertainty Principle and is open to the possibility that the universe is not deterministic.

The same problem can be seen in investments when trying to attribute performance to various factor bets in a portfolio: If we ask whether the excess return was due to a small-cap exposure, we can say "yes"; if we ask whether it was due to a low P/E exposure, we can say "yes"; if we ask whether it was due to a low beta, we can say "yes"; if we ask whether it was due to a high yield, we can say "yes"; and so on. The more one focuses on a single factor, the harder it is to disentangle the effects of the others. When new factors are found that account for excess returns, they further complicate the picture, much like when physicists find new elementary particles.

Some of you may be thinking, "Oh brother, this is snooze-ville, all this technical talk about physics." Well, did you ever consider what it's like for me at holidays? No, I thought not. I get this stuff nonstop: particle this, electron that. Or I get my uncle talking my other ear off about tax regulations. So, do I have any sympathy for you? Heck no!

Pardon me—I digress. Hang in there, dear reader. This line of thinking actually leads to some very interesting possibilities for using intuition as an investment tool. Meantime, as I got hit with physics from one side and finances from the other, I began to wonder what a physicist might make of the stock market.

CHAPTER 27

Waves and/or Particles

Don't believe for one second that atoms are made up of only stuff like protons and neutrons. I seem to recall hearing something about futons and croutons, as well.

—Steve Moris, comedian

I began looking for an opportunity to hear a physicist talk about the stock market. (I vaguely remembered from business school that the Black-Scholes option model relies on heat transfer equations from physics.) As if on cue, the next conference I attended included a presentation by Tonis Vaga—a physicist by training—on "The Coherent Market Hypothesis." This highly technical speech followed a large, sumptuous dinner and a whole day of other speakers. As a result, several of the inquiring minds around our table settled in quietly for a long winter's nap, while others collapsed audibly onto their dessert plates. My peculiar interest in the subject kept me alert and perky, like a ferret on a double espresso.

Vaga's approach is based on a framework from part of physics that examines phenomena that can exist in different states. For example, water can take a solid, fluid, or gaseous form. Another example is the electron, which can exist as a wave or a particle. One example Vaga used in his presentation was light rays, which can be emitted randomly (as in light bulbs) or coherently (as in lasers). Similarly, in Vaga's view, the stock market can exist in different states—random and efficient or concentrated and "momentum-like." The former is the conventional efficient market described in textbooks. It prices securities accurately on the basis of all known information. The risk-reward tradeoff for efficient markets is described by Sharpe's Capital Asset Pricing Model (i.e., more return for more risk). The latter state—called "coherent" by Vaga—is seen in bull and bear markets, where the market averages move powerfully in a given direction, disregarding conventional valuation measures.

In this state, the traditional risk-return tradeoff is inverted and investors can earn above-average returns with below-average risk—a heretical idea to efficient market proponents. In fact, it's an idea that only an "open" mind could entertain. Vaga postulates a third state as well, "chaotic," which represents the worst of all worlds: low return for above-average risk.

Vaga explains these different market states in terms of the interaction between fundamental and technical factors. Fundamental factors, including such variables as interest rates, company earnings, and GNP, can be bullish or bearish depending on external world events. In contrast, technical factors are sensitive to investor sentiment, which ranges between two extremes: independent, traditional thinking and "groupthink." As long as investor behavior is characterized by the former state, the market is rational and efficient. As investors become frenzied and move toward groupthink, the market state changes to coherent (if fundamentals are strongly positive or negative) or chaotic (if fundamentals are neutral).

In the coherent groupthink state, the technician's advice—"the trend is your friend"—is correct. The energy of the market has become laser-like, concentrated and powerful, and it is unwise to stand in its way. As Zweig says, "don't fight the tape." When the fundamental news is neither positive nor negative, but investors are behaving in a groupthink fashion, the market is chaotic, lunging about in fits and starts as frenzied investors exaggerate the significance of tiny bits of information. In such a state, the slightest earnings disappointment may cause violent swings in a company's stock price, regardless of long-term prospects.

Vaga calls his work an example of theory catching up with practice. One of our master investors, Marty Zweig, has established a good performance record in the face of overwhelming "evidence" from academicians that his technical analysis doesn't work. The coherent market hypothesis recognizes this fact and is broad enough to include the possibility of success from either fundamental or technical analysis, depending on the state of the market (i.e., groupthink or rational). In this sense, it also helps to resolve the investing paradox of whether one should double up on stocks that have fallen dramatically ("if you liked it at $40, you'll love it at $20!") or sell them ("cheap stocks get cheaper . . . wait until it's formed a bottom"). The resolution involves a correct reading of investor sentiment: If investor behavior is still characterized by groupthink, then yes, you should sell; if the sentiment reading indicates a rational state, however, then it's safe to double up.

The point here is not that it's always easy to determine what the sentiment reading is, but rather that either view can be appropriate, depending on investor psychology. This broader framework may help to defuse the usual catfights that ensue when "buy-cheap" fundamentalists square off with "sell-rule" technicians.

The coherent market hypothesis, with its elegant mathematics and quantitative foundation, stops short of a detailed explanation of the psychology underlying investor behavior. Vaga refers to the "Theory of Social Imitation" as the theoretical underpinning of investor groupthink. This theory examines similar behavior in nature (such as fish moving in schools or birds flying in formation) and draws comparisons between these events and societal phenomena such as fashion fads.

Interestingly, the readings recommended by my physicist cousin suggested an explanation of crowd behavior slightly different from that of social imitation. Specifically, both books suggest that modern physicists are coming to the same conclusion about physical reality that Eastern mystics have espoused for thousands of years. That is, that the ultimate reality of the physical world is not separate "balls" of matter colliding with one another, but rather an interconnected, unseparated wholeness or "oneness." To revisit a passage cited earlier, "material objects are not distinct entities, but are inseparably linked to their environment; . . . their properties can only be understood in terms of their interaction with the rest of the world." Most significantly, "[a]ccording to Mach's principle, this interaction reaches out to the universe at large, to the distant stars and galaxies" (Capra, *The Tao of Physics*, Bantam 1975). Gary Zukav, in *The Dancing Wu Li Masters* (Bantam 1979), brings this point closer to home by saying that this interconnectedness extends even to the realm of the psyche, suggesting that telepathy is not only possible but also perfectly consistent with modern physics:

> Psychic phenomena have been held in disdain by physicists since the days of Newton. In fact, most physicists do not even believe that they exist. In this sense, J. S. Bell's theorem [1964] could be the Trojan horse in the physicist's camp; first, because it proves that quantum theory requires connections that appear to resemble telepathic communication, and second, because it provides the mathematical framework through which serious physicists [all physicists are serious] could find themselves discussing types of phenomena which, ironically, they do not believe exist.

The fact that scientists were now arguing that intuition might have a scientific basis didn't completely shock me. My psychic had been predicting it all along.

CHAPTER **28**

The Case for Intuition

The power of intuitive understanding will protect you from harm until the end of your days.

—Lao Tsu

The notion of telepathy and investor groupthink brought to my mind the phenomenon of the hundredth monkey.

The *WHAT?*

The "hundredth monkey" is a shorthand name for an observed, documented event that occurred on the island of Koshima in the 1950s. Researchers on the island had dumped sweet potatoes on the beach. The monkeys they were studying there had never encountered sweet potatoes before. Although they liked the taste, the monkeys did not like the sandy coating that resulted from the potatoes lying on the beach. Eventually, one monkey genius discovered that she could clean the potatoes by washing them in the sea. Other monkeys gradually learned or copied the process until, finally, roughly 100 monkeys were washing their potatoes. Then, quite suddenly, the entire troop caught on, as if some critical mass had been reached. But more amazingly, researchers on *other islands* reported that this threshold level must have triggered the learning response in their monkeys as well, because the monkeys on those islands began using the washing technique at exactly the same time.

To explain this bizarre event, Rupert Sheldrake, a biochemist, has postulated a morphonogenetic field (M-field), which allows conveyance of information within like species (Sheldrake, *A New Science of Life*, Inner Traditions International 1995). Experiments with rats conducted by William McDougall, recreating the hundredth-monkey phenomenon, suggest that when some critical mass is reached, information enters the species' M-field (McDougall, *The Group Mind*, Ayer 1973). (This must be why I never win at Trivial Pursuit—my mind chatters the answer and the opponents pick it up.)

Dr. Larry Dossey's studies, performed with patients in hospitals, document other instances in which minds appear to have "teamed up" and become coherent (*Peace, Love and Healing: Bodymind Communication and the Path to Self-Healing*, Harper & Row 1989). Groups of people were asked to pray for certain patients, while a control group of patients had no such support. The studies indicated that the "prayer" patients recovered more rapidly. Again, there seems to be a threshold level, as with the monkeys, beyond which there is enough critical mass to help heal illness.

So, I began wondering if there is an M-field that affects investors. Are we influenced, perhaps unknowingly, to buy or sell securities because of the mindsets of investors around us? When technicians state that market sentiment is very positive, is that sentiment feeding on itself and creating a powerful M-field that convinces still more investors to buy? Is an M-field the real explanation for social imitation (i.e., fads)?

As if in response to these questions, the *Wall Street Journal* ran a front-page story with the headline: "Levitating Meditators Rely on Vibes to Bring Peace, Cut Crime, Boost Stocks" (Oct. 11, 1990). The article states that "Maharishi International University researchers say that they can show that previous waves of 'super radiance' from mass meditation have boosted the stock market." The writer of the article, knowing that *WSJ* readers are a hard-boiled bunch, goes to great lengths to show that the researchers at MIU adhered strictly to the rules of scientific method. The article quotes Bruce Russet, editor of a respected scientific quarterly: "I decided that these people had played the scientific game correctly." The MIU researchers had used sophisticated and legitimate methods for confirming their hypothesis that when a critical mass of "super radiance" is created, it can affect nonmeditators and even the stock market.

All of this may seem a bit farfetched (I warned you that we were leaving earth orbit after Chapter 20!) and largely irrelevant to everyday financial concerns. But this attitude may be changing, as excerpts from a book by Laurie Nadel, entitled *The Sixth Sense* (Prentice-Hall 1990), suggest:

- Stanford University's School of Business teaches intuition as part of its "Creativity in Business" course taught by Michael Ray and Rochelle Myers.
- Surveys show that many chief executive officers rate intuition as their most prized creative asset.
- Government experiments on intuition show that intuitive skills can be learned.

Furthermore, the Federal Reserve Bank has explored intuitive forecasting models (note: I'm not making this up): "In 1988, the Fed published a research paper titled 'The Seasonal Structure Underlying the Arrangement of Hexagrams in the *I Ching*" (Nadel, *The Sixth Sense*). The *I Ching* is a 3,000-year-old Chinese divination method; it's used like tarot cards or astrology to foretell the future. (If the Fed officials involved in this are anything like the investors I know, they probably denounced and buried this study, and then later—in the washroom—asked the author, "So, ah, where *do* you think rates are going?")

The competitive edge to be gained from honing intuitive skills could be substantial. Consider this account by Dr. Brian Weiss, chairman of the Department of Psychiatry at Mount Sinai Medical Center in Miami Beach, about a gifted patient who was able to pick winners at the racetrack: "I was both shocked and fascinated by her psychic abilities, especially the episode at the racetrack. This was tangible proof. She had the winning ticket to every race. This was no coincidence." As a result of his involvement with this patient, Dr. Weiss now says, "I listen to my dreams and intuitions. When I do, things seem to fall into place. When I do not, something invariably goes awry" (Weiss, *Many Lives, Many Masters*, Simon & Schuster 1988).

Another example from the realm of horse racing is found in Sandra Weintraub's book *The Hidden Intelligence: Innovation through Intuition* (Butterworth Heinemann 1998). She and a friend performed the following experiment at the Kentucky Derby:

> I put the name of each horse on a separate card, turned the cards over, shuffled them, and numbered them on the back side from one to ten. The names of the horses were on the underside[s] of the card[s] .... We then held each card for a few minutes, looking at the blank side of the card, until we received a mental image of the horse and its position at the finish line .... To our mutual surprise, we had chosen the same two horses to finish within the first three places.

The real surprise, though, occurred the following day, when they repeated the experiment and chose the same three horses. And how did the race actually come out?

> I had chosen the exact order of the finish for the three horses. My partner picked the same three horses, with the first two in reverse order. Considering that the race was a photo finish, it could just as easily have been his line up that predicted the winners.

Imagine the possibility of portfolio managers picking 10-baggers by using intuition alone. (And think of the reduction in overhead expenses; Ouija boards are much cheaper than computers and IT consultants.) Should we listen to our intuition as investors? It certainly was the recommendation of Bennett Goodspeed in his book *The Tao Jones Averages* (Penguin 1983), in which he advised us to "treat intuition as an equal partner with logic."

Goodspeed's advice has been heeded by researchers in computer programming, who are now developing systems to replicate intuition. They are called Artificial Neural Systems (ANS) and, in an unstructured decision environment like investing, offer distinct advantages over expert systems, which simulate deductive reasoning (i.e., logic). For example, an article by D. D. Hawley in the *Financial Analysts Journal* reported that "if an ANS could be trained to simulate the experience-based intuition of a successful technician, it could result in a substantial increase in the number of stocks that could be analyzed in real time" ("Artificial Neural Systems: A New Tool for Financial Decision Making," Nov./Dec. 1990). Although simulating inductive reasoning with computers is a long way from making psychic predictions, there is a growing interest in nondeductive decision making.

The parallels between physics and investing, such as the movement in each discipline from absolutism to relativism, are not only interesting but possibly useful for future research in finance. Tonis Vaga has used his background in physics to develop the coherent market hypothesis, which synthesizes fundamental and technical analysis into a comprehensive model of how the stock market functions. Underlying this theory is the notion that the behavior of investors moves along a continuum that ranges from rational and independent to frenzied groupthink. In practice, when groupthink dominates, the trend is your friend.

The explanation for groupthink behavior may soon be better understood because scientists are starting to accept the mind, or consciousness, as a legitimate field of study. Some modern physicists have already postulated that the ultimate physical reality is an interconnectedness of all phenomena, such that one event (a thought, for example) can affect the entire cosmos. In this framework, intuition or telepathy could become a valid tool in investing. To this end, computer scientists are working with decision-making programs that will simulate intuition.

What conclusions can be drawn from these parallels? First and foremost, it should be evident that I am not envious of my big-deal physicist cousins. We're all grownups here, and there's no need to get petty or small-minded. (But just for the record, let it be known that I had a much more active social life in both high school and college than either of them.) Second, and this is the really important point, I mean *much* more active, if you catch my drift. Third, when the hundredth Wall Street analyst likes a particular stock, chances are that the monkeys will have already cornered the market on it. Finally, don't replace TheStreet.com with a crystal ball just yet, but realize that one day experts may confirm that Shirley MacLaine has been right all along—so pay attention to your hunches. They might be worth more than your/you're thinking.

This case for intuition may strike you as interesting food for thought. But is it useful? How does it play in Peoria? Are any CEOs betting their options on it? Should Wall Street pay any attention?

CHAPTER 29

Operating on All Cylinders

I believe intuition is the sum total of all the stimuli that traders receive in an instant or over time and also the sum total of all their experience in the market.
—Howard Abell, *The Inner Game of Trading* (Irwin 1993)

In business, only intuition can protect you against the most dangerous individual of all—the articulate incompetent.
—Robert Bernstein, Chairman, Random House

Is intuition useful?

I believe that using intuition as an equal partner with logic is the single greatest strategy that money managers can employ. There, I said it. Like the Christians who were thrown to the four-legged lions, I have thrown myself before the two-legged lions who rule the major investment firms and run the markets. I can almost hear, from my office window, the sound of books slamming closed as lion investors read these sentences and exclaim, "Crackpot!"

Okay. I understand why lions would react that way. Lions rely heavily on the information that they receive from their five senses. They trust the "real" world, that which we can see and hear. They trust measurable results. They trust their experience. They trust things that they can understand. Herein lies the problem. Intuition,

by definition, is the knowing of something directly, without understanding why.

Lions dismiss this sort of knowing. They reason, "If I cannot
explain how I know something then I can't claim to know it."
Imagine a portfolio manager walking into a meeting with a pension client and saying, "I think we should sell all our Microsoft."
Immediately the client would say, "Why?" Right? We've all been
trained and conditioned to respond in that left-brained fashion.

But what if the portfolio manager simply responded, "I can't
explain why, I just know we should sell it." Well, then things would
get interesting. Side glances. Awkward throat-clearing. Patterns
interrupted on every side. Eventually, one of the clients would
remind you of the rules of the game: You must provide us with a
rationale for your investment decisions (or you can't pass "Go"
and you certainly can't collect $200!).

Imagine, though, that even in the face of this resistance our
bold portfolio manager held his ground and proclaimed, "The
intellect has little to do on the road to discovery. There comes a
leap in consciousness, call it intuition or what you will, and the
solution comes to you and you don't know how or why."

What would follow? What would happen next? Would the
pension clients scratch their heads and say, "Gee, I never thought
of it that way. Hmmm, let's give this point of view serious consideration."

Sure they would. Right after they reminded themselves that it
was "only" a few billion dollars in question. Are you kidding?!
They'd bundle him up in a straitjacket faster than you can say, "I
believe in aliens" and take him away to the silly house. The whole
incident would be relegated to the status of a humorous dinner-
party story.

Here's the interesting part, though. That crazy statement about
intellect and intuition, the one that we would probably dismiss as
nonsense, is a direct quote from Albert Einstein, arguably the best
thinker of the 20th century.

The point is obvious. In financial circles the intellect rules. That is our belief system. Wall Street is full of brilliant analysts, making huge sums of money, who have *never* demonstrated any ability to perform. Yes, they are marvelous debaters. Yes, they weave convincing arguments on any given scenario. But when we look behind their intellectual curtain, we see a little man with no magical powers of prediction. Isn't it ironic that an industry that is so obsessed with the bottom line produces so many "stars" who don't give results?

Consider the same scenario in a different industry, say, automobiles. Imagine a really smart car salesman (I hear those snickers) who gave you brilliant explanations of all the working parts of the engine and braking systems. He wowed you with his knowledge of cars. The problem, though, is that the cars he sold didn't work. Would you buy another from him? Fat chance. The product doesn't work! End of story.

Not so in the investment industry.

Interestingly, the "product" basically doesn't work. Very few firms outperform passive strategies. (Even Peter Lynch, one of our masters, who is pictured in print ads and seen on TV, might not have been able to maintain his superior record during the 1990s.) Despite the failings of the product, which is reflected in the rapid growth of index funds, there is tremendous resistance to experimenting with different approaches. In fact, in 20 years of professional investing, I've never heard a colleague suggest that we should rely more on intuition. It would be heresy. One might as well report regular Elvis sightings—they would be taken more seriously.

Still, not all the heretics are crackpots. Proponents of intuition are not all running around in the streets waving signs that proclaim, "The End is Near." In fact, in his book *The Intuitive Trader* (John Wiley & Sons 1996), Robert Koppel interviews many successful traders on the topic of intuition and its role in their strategy. Every one of the traders in the book agrees that the highest degree of expertise occurs when a person's experience and knowledge allows him to move beyond intellect into the realm of intuition. In the words of Bill Williams—a trader of 35 years and author of the book *Trading Chaos: Applying Expert Techniques to Maximize Profits* (John Wiley & Sons 1995): "At the fifth level, which is what I call the expert level, trading is almost all right hemisphere. It's all intuitive . . . . At this level you know what is the right trade without knowing how you know."

At this highest level, the intellect—which is revered by the lions who run the major investment firms—actually gets in the way of superior performance. Dr. Richard McCall, author of *The Way of the Warrior-Trader: The Financial Risk-Taker's Guide to Samurai Courage, Confidence, and Discipline* (Irwin Professional Publishing 1996), says, "The more intellectual your approach, the less you are able to be intuitive and responsive in the moment. . . . The fact is indisputable: when you really do trade well, you really cannot call it mechanical. You must be an intuitive trader!"

The paradox is that good intuition relies on lots of left-brained, intellectual experience and hard work. Edward Toppel, long-term member of the Index and Options Market and author of *Zen in the Markets* (Warner 1994), writes, "Intuition allows you to take advantage of all that hard work you've done."

Actually, this "paradox" is consistent with the message of this book: balance. A superior investor will use the skills of both the right and left brain hemispheres. The mistake that many investors make, however, is relying solely on their favorite hemisphere, the logical left side. The purpose in citing all these examples of successful intuitive traders is to encourage lion investors to experiment with using intuition, so that they will begin using all the weapons available.

"What does intuitive trading actually look like?" a lion might ask. Here is a description from Linda Leventhal, long-term independent trader and member of the International Monetary Market division of the Chicago Mercantile Exchange:

[S]ome days I'll keep trying to buy the market. I'll be trading in and out from the long side. In other words, I keep looking to buy the market on a break or retracement. All of a sudden, I'll get a feeling and I'll say to myself, this market feels heavy. That's exactly what I'll say, it feels heavy; meaning it doesn't feel right. I think it's going up. But if I rely on my intuition, my intuition tells me it feels heavy . . . it's more than just a feeling, it's vital information. If my head says buy and I keep trying to buy and it isn't working, and all of a sudden my stomach tells me it feels heavy, I will rely on my intuition. I'm going with my stomach! Most times I won't be able to even verbalize it. It just happens automatically. Experience has taught me to trust it (Koppel, *The Intuitive Trader*).

Some professional investors might react to this line of reasoning with, "Yes, but long-term investing is different from trading, therefore we shouldn't take our cues from them." My response to this comment would be that true long-term investors—the Warren Buffetts of the world—are rare these days. Portfolio managers watch their screens all day long and are ready to trade on any significant news. In this sense, they are like traders who must react in the moment to whatever stimulus is presented. In fact, portfolio managers who operate this way—trading positions on news announcements—should pay particular attention to the techniques of traders, as they are playing on the same field. Intuition would be an important ally for them.

But what about true long-term investors? Is intuition really useful to them? Again, I would argue that it is. The main difference between trading and investing is the time frame. The key to success is still the decision-making ability. The master investors discussed in this book all demonstrate the successful interplay between logic and intuition. Soros, with his penchant for reversing huge positions on a moment's notice, clearly relies heavily on his intuition. But even Buffett—the exemplary long-term investor ("My preferred investment horizon is forever")—uses intuition in his investing. He is well known for doing major business transactions only with people whom he trusts. In this sense, Buffett relies heavily on his intuitive ability to size up the character of business partners. Facts and logic (left-brain items) could help Buffett eliminate certain potential partners (the ones with shady records), but they could never confirm that someone would be trustworthy in the future. A leap of faith, based on intuition, is required for that.

Intuition also allows today's portfolio managers to operate more quickly, without assembling all the available information. Legendary investor Charles Merrill (of Merrill Lynch fame) commented on this phenomenon. He said that "if he made decisions fast—intuitively?—he was right 60 percent of the time. If he took his time and analyzed a situation carefully before reaching a decision, he would be right 70 percent of the time. However, the extra 10 percent was 'seldom worth the time'" (Weintraub, *The Hidden Intelligence*, Butterworth Heinemann 1998).

The business leaders who run the major companies in which portfolio managers invest are also recognizing the importance of intuition. Bob Galvin at Motorola is a good example: "[H]is intuition told him that wireless communication would be a gigantic opportunity for the future, although he had no strong data to support this" (Weintraub, *The Hidden Intelligence*). After a long battle with his skeptical board, Galvin prevailed. The company redirected its efforts into one of the most profitable industries in the century.

Cutting to the chase, two researchers—John Mihalsky and E. Douglas Dean at the New Jersey Institute of Technology—examined the impact of intuition on the corporate bottom line. (Let's get serious—after all, as investors, isn't the bottom line what we really care about?) They found that 80 percent of the CEOs whose profits doubled over a 5-year period were found to have above-average intuitive powers. The explanation for success? Intuitive people, as Einstein said, possess superior insight. They can reach solutions by leaps and bounds rather than waiting for all the data to be analyzed. Given the speed at which business changes these days, this trait has to rank as one of its most important assets.

In a contest that's as hard to win as investing, doesn't it seem odd that players would handicap themselves by completely ignoring this potentially extremely valuable resource? Peter Senge at MIT put it this way in his best-seller, *The Fifth Discipline* (Currency Doubleday 1990): "[Leaders] cannot afford to choose between reason and intuition, or head and heart, any more than they would choose to walk on one leg or see with one eye."

Do any modern investors take advantage of this hidden weapon? Yes. But often we don't know that they do. For obvious reasons, professional investors aren't shouting from the rooftops that they regularly consult psychics about interest rates and market levels—and yet they do. When I asked Sonia Choquette, psychic and author of four books on intuition, about her client base, she told me that nearly half of her psychic consultations are with businesspeople, many of them investors. Curious, I asked if the investors sought specific forecasts about the markets. The response: absolutely.

In our conversation, Sonia stated that the most successful investors approached it from a long-term perspective. They were in no hurry to get rich. Like Buffett, they enjoyed the process. In fact, it was more than just enjoying it; to use Sonia's words, "they love it." They were investing from the heart.

"Hmmm," I said to Sonia. "Does that mean that these investors are New Age, sentimental 'dolphin' types?"

She laughed, "Not at all. Some of them are S-O-B's of the first order! But they truly love investing."

Sonia went on to explain that these successful investors, many of them traders, were operating from passion, not fear. That seems to be the key. Fear—or its derivative, greed (which is actually fear that there won't be enough for me)—interferes with the intuitive process. Investors, therefore, need to check their motives. You don't have to start volunteering at soup kitchens, but you do have to love investing. You need to exorcise the inner Ebenezer Scrooge and replace him with the inner Warren Buffett: Mr. I-tap-dance-to-work. (Warren seems to have put the "fun" back in "fund.")

For my part, I will continue to watch with great interest as the dialectic between the right and left brain—intellect and intuition—plays itself out in the investment arena. One thing for sure, Wall Street responds to what works. Right now, the spell of reason still enjoys plenty of success. Bull markets and soaring brokerage profits don't require radical shifts. The prevailing attitude is: Don't worry, be happy.

But that may change over time. As the investing public gets wiser and more money goes into passive funds, the squeeze may be on. Investment firms will have to offer real value. They won't be able to bluff Joan Q. Public. She'll be focusing on results, not complicated theories and brilliant excuses. The intellectual smoke and mirrors, though impressive, won't matter, and certainly won't cut the mustard with disappointed investors. The majority of firms will have to admit that they can't outperform the benchmarks. The band will stop playing and Joan will take her punch bowl and go home.

When that happens, maybe, just maybe, we'll see some cracks in the armor of the intellectual fortress. Out of necessity, the lions may ask the proponents of intuition to plead their case. In fact, just recently I saw a tiny movement in this direction. The Association for Investment Management and Research (AIMR), which is to the investment community what the American Medical Association is to the medical profession, asked me to develop a talk for its members on the benefits of intuition in the investment process. You could have knocked me over with a feather. This act may symbolize the camel's nose sneaking under the tent flap.

I can imagine a day when the top investment firms understand that intellect and intuition should be in equal partnership. Left and right will be balanced. Lion Kings and Royal Wizards will team up to provide an unbeatable force.

In the meantime, if this book has given you any ideas, and you try out some of the exercises, and stretch even just a little bit, you may find a whole new dimension of the investing game opening up to you. I wish you great success as you perfect the equal partnership of left- and right-brain skills. But if you get filthy rich as the result of pure luck, hey, that's nice too! (One of my bosses used to say, "It's better to be lucky than good!") In either case, please let me know how it works for you. My e-mail address is: jimspeaks@att.net.

index

Abell, Howard, 241
Adventurer (SP) as investment temperament, 100, 103
Airline industry, 187
Allen, Woody, 25
Alpha, 226
Amabile, Teresa, 61
American Airlines, 187
American Medical Association, 248
American Productivity and Quality Center, 128, 198
American Railroad Congress, 94
Ameritrade, 95, 193
Andersen Consulting, 139
AOL, 21, 44, 195
Aristotle, 25
Art of War, The, v
Artificial Neural Systems, 239
Association for Investment Management and Research, 58, 68, 72, 85, 162, 199, 248
Aware Ego in journaling, 130–38

Bacon, Sir Francis, 214
Baldwin United, 82
Barings Bank, 104

Barron's, 37
Baruch, Bernard, 17
Batterymarch, 83
Beatles, The, 91, 94
Behavioral finance, 10, 162
Bell, Alexander Graham, 67
Bell, J. S., 234
Ben & Jerry's 3
Benson, Herbert, 41
Bernstein, Robert, 241
Bernstein, Sanford, 179
Berry, Michael, 164
Beta, 226
Bi-cameral brain, 52–54, 87, 102, 169, 208, 243, 247
Bililies, Ted, 51
Black-Scholes Options Model, 192, 231
Blockbuster Video, 193
Bogle, Jack, 171
Bohm, David, 166
Boorstin, Daniel, 162
Borders (bookstore), 37
Borg, the, 97-98
Bottom-up, as investment approach, 19

Brainstorming techniques, 206
Breadth as investment trait, 9–10.
    See also Extravert
Bridges, William, 52, 121
Brief History of Everything, A, 185
Briggs, Katherine, 23
Brinson, Gary, 68, 81, 85, 156
Brock, Woody, 186
Brown, Roger, 171
Browning, Iben, 11
Brush, Jack, 188
Buffett, Warren, 3, 4, 47, 68, 88,
    92, 102, 112, 171, 177, 204,
    245
Business Week, 225
Byrd, Admiral, 219

Calvin and Hobbes, 217
Campbell, Joseph, 171
Candid Camera, 197
Capital Asset Pricing Model, 227
Capital Group of Companies, 68
Capital Market Risk Advisors, 192
Capital Research, 69
Capra, Fritz, 227, 220, 234
Carnegie, Dale, 151
Carter, Jimmy, 26
Chanos, James, 82
Character of Organizations, The,
    121
Chartered Financial Analyst
    designation, vi
Chartered Financial Analysts (CFA),
    11, 71
Chicago Bulls, 142
Chicago Mercantile Exchange, 243
Choquette, Sonia, 247
Churchill, Winston, 25
Cleese, John, 169, 176, 199
Clients, use of MBTI with, 109–17
CML, 39
Coca-Cola, 21, 125
Coherent Market Hypothesis, 231
Color as creativity aid, 216

Complexity
    examples from master investors, 20
    as key to investment success, 15–22
Conflict, 140, 178
Confucius, 35
Consulting Psychologist Press, 60
Contrarian thinking, 179
Corporate creativity, 172
Covey, Steven, 185
Cracking creativity, 129
Crayola crayons, 215
Creativity. *See also* Intuiting
    color as aid to, 216
    corporate, 172
    "cracking," 129
    curiosity and, 61
    humor as catalyst for, 14
    as investment trait, 14
    laughter and, 61
    prayer as means to, 221
    tools for, 204
Creativity (Csikszentmihalyi), 18
Criteria for choosing investment
    "masters," 4
Cruise, Tom, 225
Csikszentmihalyi, Mihaly, 17, 200
Curiosity, 61

da Vinci, Leonardo, 17, 67
Dancing Wu Li Masters, The, 226,
    234
Data, 26
Dean, E. Douglas, 246
DeBono, Edward, 3
Decca Records, 94
Decision Traps, 166
Depth as investment trait, 13. *See
    also* Introvert
Descartes, Rene, 29
Deutsche Bank, 69
Dialogue, 165
Dickinson, Emily, 25
Dilbert, 177, 204
DiMenna, Joe, 68

Dirks, Ray, 83
Discipline, as investment trait, 12
Disney, Walt, 156
Disney World, 198, 206
Disraeli, Benjamin, 169
Diversity, 97–99, 213
Diversity training, 72–73, 127
Dividend discount models, 101, 102
Dolphins (NF), as an investment
    temperament, 105, 116
Domini Social Investments, 105
Dostoevsky, Fyodor, 12
Doyle, Ken, 108, 112, 200
Doyle, Michael, 204
Dreman, David, 100, 164
Drexel Burnham Lambert, 32
Duells, Charles, 94
Dumb and Dumber portfolio, 159
Dunning, Steve, 36
Duration, 227

Easton, Harris, Ohlson (paper by),
    228
eBay, 198
Economist Intelligence Unit, The, 59
Edison, Thomas, 41, 172, 192, 225
Efficient frontier, 226
Eight great traits. *See* Traits of
    investment masters
Einstein, Albert, 6, 13, 169, 171,
    225, 230, 246
Ellis, Charles, 226, 227
Embracing Your Inner Critic, 130
EMDR therapy, 54
Emerson, Ralph Waldo, 27, 139
Emotions, 43
Ethics, 112
eToys, 44, 58, 197
Extravert (Breadth),
    exercises for strengthening, 36
    as investment trait, 24–25, 111

Farrelly, Gail, 59
Federal Reserve Bank, 237

Feeling (F), as investment personality
    trait, 84, 90–91, 111
Feeling (Passion)
    exercises for strengthening, 42
    as investment trait, 28
Feynman, Richard, 13
Fifth Discipline, The, 166, 247
Filters, for teamwork, 86–88
Financial Analysts Journal, 59, 170,
    186, 239
First Chicago, 81
Fisher, David, 68
Flexibility
    as investment trait, 15
    exercises for strengthening, 44–45
Forbes, 14
Ford, Henry, 86, 89
Fortuna, Phil, 229
Fortune, 37, 108
Foxes, as investment temperament,
    103, 116, 177
Frank Russell Company, 58
Franklin Mutual Series Fund, 69
Frasier, 31
Freedman, Jay, 166
Friday, Sgt. Joe, 27
Frost, Robert, 32
Funt, Alan, 197
*Future of Investment Management,
    The*, 58, 72

Gandhi, Mohandas, 29, 112
Gates, Bill, 95
Gekko, Gordon, 15, 113, 193, 195
General Electric, 155
General Mills, 155
*General Theory of Employment and
    Interest, The*, 98
Gerard, Glenna, 161
Goldberg, Natalie, 154
Golden gloves ethics, 112
Golden rule ethics, 112
Goldman Sachs, 48
Goodspeed, Bennett, 239

Gough, 60
Group Mind, The, 236
Grove, Andy, 27
Guardian (SJ), 100–102
Guide to the Development and Use of the Myers-Briggs Type Indicator, 60
Guitar, as image of dynamic tension in groups, 92
Gurdjieff, 215
Gutenberg, Johann, 192

Habits, 3
Haman, Gerald, 155
Harris Associates, 171
Harvard Business Review, 61
Hawley, D. D., 239
Heart of Conflict, The, 70
Hedge funds, 104
Hegel, 185
Heisenberg Uncertainty Principle, 226
Heroes, creative, 148
Hidden Intelligence, The, 156, 238, 246
Hill, Lee, 221
Holmes, Sherlock, 10, 20
How to Kill Creativity, 61
How to Make Meetings Work, 204
Hulbert, Mark, 163
Hulbert Financial Digest, 163
Humor as catalyst for creativity, 14
Hundredth monkey phenomenon, 235

I Ching (ancient oracle), 237
IBM, 193
Idealist (NF), 100, 105. *See also* Dolphins
Index and options market, 243
Inner Game of Investing, The, 48
Inner Game of Trading, The, 241
Inquiry circle, 152
Insanity, definition of, vi, 3
Interaction Associates, 70, 81–82, 88, 147, 149, 172, 204, 207

Internal critic, 129–38, 216
International Monetary Market, 243
Introvert (Depth)
  exercises for strengthening, 36
  as investment trait, 24–25
Introverted (I), as investment personality trait, 110, 208
Intuiting, 26, 39. *See also* Creativity
Intuitive (N)
  as investment personality trait, 85, 86, 89, 138, 172, 205, 221
  linked to creativity, 59–60, 93
Intuitive Trader, The, 243
Investment masters, 4. *See also* Buffett, Warren; Lynch, Peter; Soros, George; Wanger, Ralph; Zweig, Martin
  traits of, 9–16, 21

Jackson, Phil, 142
James, William, 219
Janus Fund, 68, 177
Janus Global Technology Fund, 21
Jefferson, Thomas, 129
Jenner, Edward, 170
Jesus, 218
Jordan, Michael, 4, 48, 69
Journaling, 130–38
Judging (Discipline)
  exercises for strengthening, 44
  explained as investment trait, 30
Judging (J), as investment personality trait, 45, 51, 84, 91, 114, 172, 184, 205, 209
Jung, Carl, 52, 63, 147, 156, 216, 218

Kant, Immanuel, 32
Karaoke, 155
Kasparov, Gary, 57
Keirsey, David, 97, 99
Kekulé, 217
Kellogg Graduate School of Management, 173
Kelvin, Lord, 94

Kennedy, John F., 24
Kentucky Derby, 238
Keynes, John Maynard, 98
Kidder Peabody, 166
King Solomon, 196
King, Billie Jean, v
King, Martin Luther, 29, 112
Koppel, Robert, 243
Krishnamurti, J., 75
Krueger, Otto, 56
Kruger, W., 36

L.A. Confidential, 76
Lance, Bert, 28
Lao Tsu, 235, 81
Larsen, Earnie, 3
Laughter, 61
Learning Maps, 206
LeBaron, Dean, 59, 83
Leeson, Nick, 104
Left-right brain theory. *See* Bi-
    cameral brain
Legg Mason, 103
Lennon, John, 32
Leventhal, Linda, 243
Levitt, Arthur, 164
Lewis, C. S., 175
Lewis and Clark, 177
Limited, The, 38
Lincoln, Abraham, 203
Lions (SJ)
    as investors, 100–101, 177, 188, 247
    as leaders, 55
    as STJ personalities, 52, 114, 121,
        123, 140, 161
Livermore, Jesse, 12, 83
Loeb, Gerald, 94, 226
Lone Ranger, 196
Lu, Mike, 21, 22
Lynch, Peter, 12, 36–37, 42, 47, 69,
    88, 104, 159, 243

Machiavelli, 77
Mach's principle, 234

MacLaine, Shirley, 240
Magic Eye, 18
Maguire, Jerry, 27
Maharishi International University,
    236
*Managing Investment Firms: People
    and Culture,* 68, 85
Mankind Project, The, 144, 151
Many Lives, Many Masters, 238
Markowitz, Harry, 226
Masters. *See* Investment masters
MBTI. *See* Myers-Briggs Type
    Indicator
McCall, Dr. Richard, 243
McCormick, Charles, 195
McDougall, William, 236
Meditation, 41, 236
Memories, Dreams, and Reflections,
    147
Mencken, H. L., 157
Mensa, 158
Merck, 19
Merrill Lynch, 48, 69, 170, 246
Merrill, Charles, 246
Michelangelo, 169, 176
Michalko, Michael, 129
Microsoft, 21, 198, 242
Mihalsky, John, 246
Miller, Bill, 103
Millikan, Robert, 94
MIT, 247
Modern Portfolio Theory, 226
Money Game, The, v
Moore, Robert, 52, 144
Moris, Steve (comedian), 30, 231
Morningstar, 108
Morphonogenetic field, 236
Mount Sinai Medical Center, 238
Muldoon, Brian, 70
Munger, Charlie, 14, 68, 102
Music composition, 219
Myers, Isabel, 23
Myers-Briggs Type Indicator
    for diagnosing investor traits, 23–34

Myers-Briggs Type Indicator
  (continued)
  preferences explained, 23
  use with clients, vi, 110
  for U.S. presidents, 53
  Website for on-line test, 34

Nadel, Laurie, 237
New Jersey Institute of Technology,
  246
New Madrid earthquake, 11
New Science of Life, A, 236
New Testament, 218
New York Times, The, 36, 154, 165
Newton, Isaac, 58
Newtonian physics, 226
Niederman, Derrick, 48
Niednagel, Jonathan, 47
Nietzsche, Friedrich, 191
Nixon, Richard, 24
NordicTrack, 37

Objectivity as investment trait, 10.
  See also Thinking
Ockham, 162
Odd Couple, The, 31, 44
O'Donnell, Patrick, vi, 70, 72, 85
Olson, Ken, 94
One Group Mutual Funds, 69
Open Space Technology, 121
Open Space Technology: A User's
  Guide, 122
Oppenheimer, Robert, 229
Overconfidence, 10, 36, 164
Owen, Harrison, 121, 207
Owls (NT), as investment
  temperament, 102, 115

PaineWebber, 11
Palm Pilots, 194
Pascal, Blaise, 13
Passion, as investment trait, 15. See
  also Feeling
Patton, George, 29, 112, 125

P/E ratios, 101, 188, 209
Perceiving (Flexibility)
  exercises for strengthening, 44
  explained as investment trait, 30
Perceiving (P), as investment
  personality trait, 46, 84, 91,
  114, 172, 184, 205
Phar Mor, 43
Phillips, Michael, 58
Physics, similarities to investing,
  226–30
Pierce, Ambrose, 29
Pokémon, 194
Portraits of Temperament, 97, 99,
  110
Prayer, 221
Preferences (in MBTI), 23
Presidents, 53
Presley, Elvis, 243
Price, T. Rowe, 94, 227
PriceWaterhouseCoopers, 59
Prisoner's dilemma, 75
Progroff, Ira, 216
Putnam, vi, 70
Pzena, Richard, 179

Quakers, 41

Rahl, Leslie, 192
Rain Man, 225
Random House, 241
Rationalist (NT), as investing
  temperament, 100, 102
Ray, Michael, 237
Records, investment masters'
  performance, 4
Recovery, 12-step programs, 146,
  152
Risk, 227
Robert's Rules of Order, 54
Robinson, Alan, 172
Roethke, Theodore, 170
Rogers, Will, 30
Rothenberg, James, 69

Russett, Bruce, 237
Russo, J. Edward, 166

S&P 500, 21, 92, 103, 105, 108, 166
Sacred Hoops, 142
Samuels, Mina, vii
Samurai, 162
Schoemaker, Paul H., 166
Schweitzer, Albert, 109
*Science and the Common
    Understanding*, 229
Scrooge, Ebenezer, 248
Scudder, Stevens & Clark, 229
SEC, 164
Sees Candy stores, 14
Senge, Peter, 121, 166, 247
Sensing (Observation)
    exercises for strengthening, 39
    explained as investment trait, 26
Sensing (S), as investment
    personality trait, 51, 85, 86, 89,
    110, 165, 172, 205, 209, 221
Serious Creativity, 3
*Seven Habits of Highly Effective
    People, The*, 186
Shakespeare, William, 67, 193
Shaw, George Bernard, 157
Sheldrake, Rupert, 236
Sherrerd, Katrina, 59
Simpson, Homer, 173, 177
Sixth Sense, The, 237
Skinner, B.F., 171
Slimfast, 3
Smith, Adam, v
*Social Meaning of Money and
    Property, The*, 108
Soros, George, 10, 12
South Africa (bank), 92
Southwest Airlines, 187
Sovran Bank, 92
Sperry, Roger, 52, 156
Stage II Recovery, 3
Stanford University, 237
Star Trek, 26, 29, 44

Star Wars, 185
State Street Global Advisors, 69
Statman, Meir, 199
Stern, Sam, 172
Stevenson, Robert Louis, 32
Stone, Hal, 130, 216
Stone, Sidra, 130, 216
Straus, David, 204
Streetlamp syndrome, v
Sun Tzu, v

Tao Jones Averages, The, 239
Tao of Physics, The, 226, 227, 229,
    234
Taos, New Mexico, 154
Teamwork, 84–88
Temple Inland, 195
Terrell, Steven, 92
Tesla, Nikola, 26
TheStreet.com, 240
Thinking (Objectivity)
    exercises for strengthening, 42
    explained as investment trait, 28
Thinking (T), as investment
    personality trait, 51, 74, 75, 85,
    86, 111, 165, 205
Thinkubator, The, 155
Thompson, Chic, 61
3M, 198
Three Musketeers, The, 89
Time Inc., 195
Times Mirror, 195
Tips on the Creative Life, 213
*Tomorrow's Leading Investment
    Managers*, 59
Tools for creativity, 204
Top-down, as investment approach,
    19
Toppel, Edward, 243
Toys 'R' Us, 57–58
Tracking error, 226
*Trading Chaos: Applying Expert
    Techniques to Maximize Profits*,
    243

Treynor, Jack, 170
Traits of investment masters
    explained, 9–16
    as used by Mike Lu, 22
Tversky, Amos, 162
Twain, Mark, 9, 175
Type Talk at Work, 56

Ueland, Brenda, 213
Uline Corporation, 30
United Airlines, 187
University of Chicago, 139

Vaga, Tonis, 231
Van der Rohe, Mies, 27
Van Gundy, Arthur, 155
Venture Capital, 104
Voice dialogue, 130–38, 216

Wall Street (movie), vi, 113, 193,
    195
Wall Street Journal, 57, 69, 82, 101,
    103, 236
Wanger, Ralph, 10, 14, 102, 171

Warner, Harry, 94
Warner Brothers, 195
Washington Post, 195
Watterson, Bill, 217
Way of the Warrior Trader, 243
Weintraub, Sandra, 156, 238, 246
Wheatley, Meg, 121
Whitehead, Alfred North, 23
Wiess, Brian, 238
Wilber, Ken, 185, 186
Williams, Bill, 243
Williams, Robin, 24
Wilson, Woodrow, 191
Winning on Wall Street, 12
Wooly Bully, 163
Worth, 21
Worth On-line, 38
Writing Down the Bones, 154

Zebra in Lion Country, A, 10
Zeikel, Arthur, 170
Zen, 161
Zen in the Markets, 243
Zweig, Martin, 12, 45, 68, 100, 232